A TWELVE-STEP
SELF-
TRANSFORMATION

a t t a i n i n g   p h y s i c a l ,   m e n t a l ,
s p i r i t u a l ,   a n d   e m o t i o n a l   s o b r i e t y

w i t h   M A R K   H .   a n d   F L O Y D   H .

ISBN: 0-9760184-0-3
Printed in the United States of America
Henderson Books, Publisher & Distributor

A NOTE TO THE READERS ABOUT BILL W.'s OBSERVATIONS REGARDING A FOUR-FOLD ILLNESS

In his later talks, Bill W. spoke not about a two-fold illness or a three-fold illness but he discussed alcoholism's four-fold nature. He identified what he saw as the four levels of sobriety: physical sobriety, mental sobriety, spiritual sobriety and the final level of sobriety he discussed: emotional sobriety. In our book, the cover recognizes those four levels. It also illustrates the journey of the two authors from the darkness to the light. The "greater than" symbol (>) was chosen to illustrate their experience: each time we attain another level of sobriety, we feel *greater than* we did in the prior stage(s). Thus, the cover depicts the goal of this book: to share with others the four-fold solution that the authors found on their four-part journey that moved them degree by degree from the darkness to the light as they pursued *all four* levels of sobriety. The authors hope that their experience might help any others who choose to seek all four levels of healing that Bill W. identified for us.

ABOUT THE BOOK

A Twelve-Step Journey to SELF-Transformation recounts the authors' early days together after they met in a fellowship, but it is not limited to recounting the spiritual experiences they shared in that aspect of their lives. Though the authors do focus on their own personal experiences in working the steps together and then with others, they also share the events that occurred *beyond* that part of their lives. It would be those events that led, in fact, to further healing on three other levels.

While we divided our book into parts to share our experiences in seeking the four levels of healing and sobriety discussed by Bill W., we found that no real divisions exist. All in this manifestation, we discovered in our case, is but one whole. That required for us a holistic treatment approach to bring about healing and to give us all four levels of sobriety.—Mark and Floyd

(Please note: The authors do not intend for this book to be a replacement for any approved literature.)

Dedicated by Mark
(10-19-82)
to
"The Way"

Dedicated by Floyd
(7-11-89)
to
Ashley, My Daughter
and to Marie, for identifying the mental and emotional and physical work that I needed—even after my life-saving spiritual work

MARK H.'S ACKNOWLEDGMENTS

I wish to acknowledge the people who have shown me love over the years as I have continued to go through the process of transformation, including Clark, Jerry, Jack, Tom, Dave, Bruce, Macri, Shorty, John, TeeHee, Jeff, Dan, Roger, Bill, JoAnn, Sherri, Marsha, Big John, Dino, Rocky, Jeremy, Robert B., Julie, Dave F., Vadim, Peter M., Tommy B., Tom N., Rich W. and Chris R.;

For Guidance, thanks to Don, Joe, Jack, Floyd, Merton, Maharaj, DeMello, Big Frank, and Saint Benedict;

For my Physical and Mental Health, thanks to Marie, Andrea, Joan, Mimi, and Kathleen.

FLOYD H.'S ACKNOWLEDGMENTS

To Wayne P. and Tommy A. for time and effort in the early stages;

To Mark for his guidance through the spiritual part of my work;

To Joan, Marie, and Andrea for sharing their expertise in the treating of my physical, mental, and emotional needs;

To Sri Nisargadatta Maharaj, for shedding light on the false selves and thus guiding me to transformation through full awareness of the True *SELF*.

Finally, we thank Brandon Tran for the professional work he did on our websites. He can be reached at btran@intmarketing.net.

*

PART ONE

THE SPIRITUAL

*

CHAPTER 1

"THE MAN ON THE COUCH"

The picture that Mark presented while seated on the couch in a condominium in Denver, Colorado was in direct contrast to the conditions outside. Just beyond the door, the skies were a calm blue, the summertime sun felt warm to those walking beneath its rays, and both plants and people outside were blooming handsomely. Inside, by contrast, Mark was *not* calm and light. He was disturbed and dark. Rather than experiencing a sense of blooming and thriving, he felt as if he were shriveling up and dying. He could not see life blooming all about him, but he *could* see ending his own life.

The searing spiritual and emotional and physical and mental anguish that had burned away his will to live was beyond belief. He should be happy, joyous, and free—sitting in a lovely condo in a lovely state on a lovely day. At forty-four years of age, he had been sober since age thirty-four. Having suffered the slings and arrows of outrageous alcoholism, surely with ten years away from his last drink he could be nothing *but* happy, joyous and free. At least most so concluded, anyway; yet here he sat—depressed beyond belief, suffering a pain in every cell of his body. He had no job, no money, and no prospects for a future. He sat totally immobilized. Mark at the adult age of forty-four, following all of his very best efforts for the past ten years, found himself unable to walk outside his condo because of his overwhelming pain and fear. He could not move into the light, could not experience the calm, and certainly could not bloom.

This was not how his life was supposed to turn out. He had an advanced degree along with goals and dreams and hopes, but now they were all as far removed from Mark as he was distanced from himself—from his True *SELF*. At the midday point of a bright, summertime day in the mountains of Colorado, Mark was instead in the middle of the Dark Night of the Soul. That shadowy night proffered no hope, no future, no pleasant thoughts of the past, no pleasant forecast for a future, no God, and no self-reliance. That darkness could seemingly provide him nothing, in fact, that could make available a life worth living. With the ignored light all about, he could see only the path of darkness, the path of suicide that seemed to him to be the only sensible route to take. He could not walk outside, but he felt he *could* walk that black passageway to its end...to his end.

Sober for ten years at the time he ended up on that couch, he had enjoyed an improved life sometime prior to this point. That life had risen from a heap of ashes, so for six of his ten years without a drink, he had enjoyed the benefits: a good job, a wife, a home purchased along with its accompanying mountain property and a host of friends. But the past four years of his journey had delivered him into a lethal frame of mind. From the couch this day he reviewed how all those benefits of sobriety had evaporated like the morning mist rising from the nearby lake. *What had happened?* he wondered. *What was this incredible pain about that had taken over? What is wrong with me?* he asked. In spite of all his work to produce hope, in spite of all the work with his disciplines, in spite of countless meetings with support groups notwithstanding, he had found no real or lasting solution. His present mindset constructed but one resolution to his predicament: *Mark, you must end your life.*

Then I shall, he answered.

Having made from the depths of the darkness his decision, Mark's next awareness would be of a bright light: *I've done it. I'm free. I'm experiencing what they said I would experience. The light. The beautiful brightness of lovely radiance.* Further adjustment of his eyes after squinting reflexively to block out the illumination left Mark aware that he was not soaring to some celestial retreat but was instead in a very-much-man-made room. Having failed even in his desire to end it all, a chain of events that some Higher Power or Consciousness had set into motion unfolded in a way that—days after having left that Colorado couch—allowed Mark to find himself locked away in a psychiatric hospital in Houston, Texas. After some initial disappointment that the final escape to a heavenly haven had been denied him, he eventually became grateful to be in the hospital, for that location marked the beginning point of the next leg of a journey that would eventually result in Mark's crossing the path of a man named Floyd. At the time Mark would meet him, Floyd could have easily been confused with *the Mark* who had been sitting in the depths of despair on a couch in a condo in Four Corners.

Only because of the changes that ultimately began to transform Mark's thinking and thus his perceptions about life, about himself, about others, and about that incredible thing called the *present moment* would Floyd be drawn to him when the latter reached that same state of darkness from which Mark had been extracted. How did it happen? What are the important details that can explain such an alteration as Mark's...and later Floyd's? How was it that Mark came to help others in a similar mental condition to be extracted as well?

Mark would ask Floyd one day, "Have you ever felt the way I described, the way I felt as I sat on the couch that day?" *Yes.* "Have you ever thought to yourself that perhaps your society, parents, teachers, books, television, and all the other influences that have shaped our belief systems were askew, were wrong?" *No.* "Have you so much as even considered the possibility that, in fact, your belief systems are designed to lead you to great suffering?" *No.* Then Mark explained, "Only when I began to suspect all of it, and to evaluate all of my experiences through an impartial questioning of every idea and emotion and belief I held, did a course of action begin to change and transform me." The entire process he would reveal one day in the future when he co-wrote a book through which the process could be documented and shared with others.

You now hold that book.

Mark left the hospital and moved to a small town in the Hill Country of Texas and began a journey from 1991 to the present that is at best difficult to put into words. A journey of *SELF*-transformation occurred—a journey in which the "false self" died and the True *SELF* emerged. His would be a passage in which past trauma would finally be addressed; when destructive and ineffective belief systems that he had incorporated into his life from a crazy and insane world would be abandoned; when the development of a practical approach that he could use to undergo a radical *transformation* could begin to be revealed to him...and would later be revealed *through* him.

You the reader hold in your hand the book that will reveal the process, and it will not disclose the method in the usual, expository fashion by explaining. Instead, this book will use a unique approach, an experiential approach, so that one will not just *read* about what happened but will actually *experience* the process as it unfolds on these pages. Mark's transformation began in earnest when he began to follow in earnest the clear-cut path of instructions which are laid out in approximately two-hundred words that carry one through a series of a dozen steps. His transformation culminated when the additional steps that he took beyond those twelve lifted him even higher.

The transformation bloomed as he rigorously and intently pursued an awareness of the false for the next two years; eventually, the transformation matured after he saw the false and began differentiating that from the truth. Ultimately, he would incorporate a daily meditation life into his daily life; he would study other disciplines of spiritual thought and practices; and most of all he simply began to do what was revealed to him by his working mind.

Suddenly, changes begin to manifest in his life. The man on the couch would become the man on the tape, a tape heard by Floyd when he had reached a deep state of despair from which he had no hope of escape. In Mark's restored condition, Floyd would find a man capable of helping him differentiate the true from the false. That would be the beginning of Floyd's shift that would eventually move him away from insanity and past his pain. Subsequent actions would transport him through the healing process, would prepare his mind for the awakening, and would eventually fix him in a state of permanent peace wherein he could enjoy a life of Living in the Moment, fixed in The Eternal Now. He would finally shift from living the life of a warrior—constantly engaging in one battle after another—to reveling in a life truly lived from a position of neutrality.

CHAPTER 2

"THE MAN ON THE TAPE"

Scientists speak of parallel universes. Geometry talks of parallel lines—lines running an equal distance apart at all points and never touching. Sometimes there are distant lives that seem to run a parallel course but occasionally…they just happen to touch.

The picture Floyd presented while seated on the side of his bed in a five-bedroom, three-bath home situated on a double-sized lot was paralleling the conditions outside. Outside, the October skies were dark, the weather was cold, and nothing was thriving at all. Inside, Floyd was also dark and cold. He enjoyed no sensation of thriving but suffered an overwhelming sense of despair instead. Life seemed useless, worthless, and better ended than extended.

The four thieves—spiritual agony, emotional agony, physical agony, and mental agony—had stolen his will to live though he should have been happy, joyous, and free—sitting in a beautiful home on a cool Halloween night, seven-and-a-half years away from his last drink. At more than forty-nine years of age and dry since forty-two, he nevertheless sat in a black state of depression of a depth beyond comprehension to most. Floyd, despite all of his very best efforts, found himself no longer able to endure his overwhelming pain. *You need the strength to end it all*, his thinking mind said.

This was not how his life was supposed to have turned out. He had several advanced degrees and several prosperous businesses, but something was missing in spite of what most took to be an ideal life. If a wilderness was literally "a place to be passed through," his debilitated state had left him in the middle of a wasteland-of-a-life. He could see no hope of ever coming out the other side in one piece. He had reached a point where he felt as if he were a pane of glass, held in the hands of the world. He felt as if the thumbs of the masses were pushing so hard that they had bent him totally out of shape, putting him under so much strain that if anyone happened to apply even the slightest additional pressure, he'd shatter into a million pieces. He lifted his head only enough to look outside at the darkness, and he realized that even at noon on the brightest day, a similar darkness was all that he could see. Just darkness...and more darkness. The path of suicide seemed the most logical route to follow to his thinking mind that night.

Dry for those seven-plus years, Floyd nevertheless had gained no true peace. Unanswered questions led to a continuing sense of incompletion and Floyd felt inside as if he were living The Great Lie. He now sat galvanized into a state of immobility. *What's wrong with me?* he asked himself. In spite of all his work and countless meetings with his support group, he had not found himself—his True *SELF*. In that torn state of duality in which "he" could ask a question of "himself" and in which "he" had not found "himself," the best that his mindset offered as a resolution to his predicament was, *Floyd, if this is as good as it's going to get, you may as well end it now.*

Then I shall, he answered. He had not been fortunate enough to meet someone with whom he could journey beyond that "he-himself" duality and transform into a state of wholeness that comes in knowing the True *SELF*. Yet even in that plan to end his life he failed. In spite of being years away from his last drink, Floyd continued to flounder.

He had received contradictory statements throughout all the years about what his condition was and what he needed to treat it. As the inconsistencies continued, he became more confused than ever, but that was about to change. A chain of events began unfolding which put into his hands a copy of a tape on which a man was offering a clear-cut course of action that Floyd had not yet taken. Indeed, the man on the tape erased much of the confusion as he offered a clear message of consistency, and Floyd felt there might be hope that he could end his suffering...*and* still live.

The tape began with, "Hi, my name's Mark H. and I'm a real alcoholic." Then the man proceeded to speak truths not heard before by Floyd, truths that aligned with the original message. These truths he was hearing were rooted in the teachings of the founders of a program that in its early days experienced a greater than 90% success rate but by Floyd's time had a greater than 90% failure rate, according to some studies. Suddenly, Floyd sat up as he listened. A glimmer of hope came into his being as he continued listening to the man on the tape.

Hearing that tape marked the beginning of a journey that would eventually result in great effort to find the man on the tape, a man who would see in Floyd a former picture of himself when he once sat in the depths of despair on a couch in a condo in the Four Corners area of the U.S. Only because of the changes that had already manifested in Mark would Floyd be drawn to him when the latter reached that same state from which Mark had been extracted. The parallels in the lives of two who had never met were amazing. The parallels in the effects of their working the steps would be remarkable. And the parallels in the additional steps that both would have to take after the first twelve would also prove to be astonishingly similar.

To begin the journey, Mark would guide Floyd through a process that would eventually lead to his joining his guide in the writing of a book that described the events that led to their initial stage of freedom. A journey of *SELF*-transformation occurred in Floyd just as it had in Mark, a journey in which Floyd would see all the false selves that blocked his knowing Who He Really Is. The journey and work and effort with the steps ended in attaining that state of Realization, of coming to know The Great Reality after having been shown by Mark all the great falsehoods that Floyd had taken to be truth. Freedom began to come as Floyd got free of all the false belief systems that had been programmed into him and when he found who he was not in order to be able to know Who He Really Is. The next three levels of freedom the two men would also find together as they sought the additional treatment needed by both in order to gain freedom in the other areas that Bill W. spoke of—freedom in the physical area, freedom in the mental area, and freedom from the emotional elements of alcoholism as well. This is the story of their journey to Four-Fold Healing.

CHAPTER 3

"MARK FIRST THOUGHTS"

In another book, a man named Lazarus had died and his body had been bound in cloths and placed in a tomb. In that account, he was brought back to life; then the one who returned him to life turned to certain agents—or disciples—and said, "Unbind him, and set him free." A power allowed one to be reborn, but humans were used afterwards to set him free that he might enjoy abundantly his second chance at life. Such happens on a daily basis as recovered alcoholics unbind those still suffering from the ravages of this disease. In this book, you will see that scenario played out in a first-hand account in the pages that follow.

Several types of people might benefit from a reading of our book: first, the person who is using alcohol and is wondering if a problem might be developing with its use; or, two, a person who has such a drinker in his or her life—be it a husband, a wife, a daughter, a son, any other relative, or a friend. Third, anyone who is sponsoring or who wants to sponsor and who might consider using some additional aids will find those in this book which contains two different methods for working the steps to help the different types of people who seek help. Anyone addicted to anything that we humans become addicted to will find help in these pages, we believe. Finally, those can be helped who have been dry or clean for years but who sense that more is still needed, that something still seems to be missing.

We hope all might benefit from our sharing of our failed

attempts to use alcohol effectively and from seeing the spiritual experiences and subsequent steps that we took that led to our recovery from this fatal and progressive disease. Those who love someone who abuses alcohol might come to a better understanding of the disease and the behaviors that it inspires through reading this book. That includes approximately 80% of the people in the United States who might benefit from going through this work. If we were to add to that number the total of those whose lives will be adversely affected directly or indirectly by alcohol, nearly every American (indeed, nearly everyone worldwide) can find something beneficial here.

How do we know anything about this universal problem? Because we were two drunks who spread misery, pain, and destruction while in the throes of the disease. Proud of that? No, but we are living in the joy of God's Grace today. How might we help with this universal problem? God has blessed us by putting into our lives his agents who have helped us to repair our broken relationships with God, others, and ourselves. Proud about that? No, but we are living in the serenity of the deep gratitude we feel for God having saved our lives and for agents unbinding us from the shackles of this disease.

If the sharing of our failures, our spiritual experiences and the strength and hope that we have gained in recovery can aid the smallest fraction of people affected by alcoholism, we will feel something positive has come forth.

In the upcoming pages, you will see an alcoholic relive certain episodes during the most traumatic days of his drinking career. I met him after he had passed through the stages of being a social drinker, a moderate drinker, a hard drinker. I met him when he had become a full-blown, *real alcoholic*. To relive those episodes was not easy for him as he reconstructs for you the events that could be today the most embarrassing moments of his life. Then why open up to reveal the horrors of his behavior? Why would he expose the sick thinking that characterized his mind even as he thought he was right and the rest of the world was wrong? Why would he lay himself bare for any who are the type to judge or criticize him for his past?

For one reason: to give hope to others who are there or who may be headed there and to help himself by remembering what it was like so that he might not ever return there. He also wants to offer hope to people living with such miserable creatures. If he changed, maybe the suffering people whom others care about can change. There is also something about being relieved of suffering that inspires one to risk all for others. Thus, Floyd will risk all in recounting events from his most humiliating days.

The episodes described may be worse than, or not nearly as bad as, episodes in the lives of the reader or your loved ones. But a thread of commonality will be recognized if the reader is dealing with a *real alcoholic*. In the best case, the reader might receive a glimpse of what the future might be like when the alcohol quits "working," for the effects (as well as the disease itself) are both progressive and fatal.

Should you feel that the tone, the crudeness, or the behavior described in some scenes is too offensive, we beg you to read on anyway, for it is our desire that the reader might gain hope in seeing that seemingly impossible (in fact, totally horrible, totally disgusting, totally insane) attitudes, ideas and behaviors can change. Following the descriptions of the actual events that occurred in the life of one alcoholic, I will offer an analysis of the behavior to explain to the reader exactly what we can see in the conduct of the problem drinker but that the *real alcoholic* cannot see about herself or himself. The analysis of the behavior of the alcoholic that I helped unbind will provide deeper insight and understanding into the cunning, baffling, and powerful disease that so negatively affects such huge portions of the world's population.

After that analysis in each step, I will offer the kind of advice that I have given to help thousands recover from this disease. We hope that the advice offered will help those who are suffering to realize what they must do to recover. We also hope that our work will provide those who are dealing with alcoholics some additional tools which they might use in working with others. And we hope this book will allow those who have a loved one suffering from the disease to understand better both the disease and the possi-bilities for recovery. We see miracles and we see tragedies on a daily basis. We see death and we see rebirth on a daily basis. Our prayer is this book might help guide all affected toward a miracle, toward rebirth.

Floyd and I recount in the following pages our experiences together and we speak to all who are interested in going through life awake, aware, and conscious. We will not merely *discuss* how we work the steps. Instead, we will actually *demonstrate* the use of certain tools in the hope that this book might help some pick up those tools and use them as well.

Although our experience of the steps comes from our being *real alcoholics*, all persons can achieve a spiritual experience and a spiritual awakening if they will take the actions in these steps. God's Grace falls equally on all. Those who choose to seek God through a specific course of actions will experience God mani-festing through them.

The choice is yours to make; it can be made for you by nobody else. Do it because you want to; do it because you want to be involved in creating a new life; and do it because you no longer want to live with the effects of your past creations. Remember that all of our troubles are of our own making. There are no victims.

The only problem with embracing this concept is that it makes you fully responsible for your life. But isn't the thought of that exciting?! By working the steps, we experience more and more our new reality—The Great Reality—and we begin to remember more and more Who We Really Are as we lose more and more of who we are not.

I would also like our readers to understand that this book is not *gender specific* or *God specific*. Where I use "Him" and "He" and "God," I could as easily use "Her" or "She" or "Goddess" or any other terms offered in the literature to point toward that Higher Power required for recovery. The names are not important. Our intent is simply to provide the reader with some tools to be used in having a spiritual experience and a spiritual awakening.

I encourage our readers, prior to further reading, to write out a prayer in which you ask the God of your own conception to lay aside what you think you know about God, about any step program, about your "disease," or about the disease of a loved one and to give you an open mind and heart. Only then can you have a new experience with truth as it is revealed to you. May God bless you and keep you. Mark.

CHAPTER 4

"FLOYD'S FIRST THOUGHTS"

In the upcoming pages, you will see me relive certain episodes in my "drinking career." Should you find some scenes offensive, I beg you to read on anyway, for it is our desire that the reader might gain hope in seeing that seemingly insane attitudes and behaviors *can* change. Following each of the personal accounts that provide a glimpse into scenes from a past life embroiled in the depths of alcoholism and addiction, Mark analyzes the behaviors to explain their origins. Then, he will offer the type advice he has given as a counselor or spiritual advisor to help thousands recover from a seemingly hopeless state of sick bodies and sick minds. Proofreaders of the manuscript testified one after another that this book helped guide them to a wonderful place, to a sense of rebirth. The man who typed the final draft said, "I should pay you two, considering what I got from reading this book as I typed it." (We pursued that offer, but he took the check anyway.)

Secondly, I want to endorse something that came from Mark's non-judgmental and open-minded nature that made all the difference to me. Mark has said that references to a Higher Power in this book are not *gender specific* or *God specific*. For reasons I'll reveal later, I can testify that had he not been willing to allow that approach for me, nothing more could have happened. Through eventual experiences in working with others, I found that many who were abused as children by certain people must be given the option set forth by Bill W. in the literature. I have since found that many in the fellowship had experiences similar to mine and could not progress unless truly allowed to choose a God of their own conception.

So why did I need Mark after years without a drink and after years of devoted, sincere work? In the beginning of my journey, I had joined the fellowship for six months and left, the format having awakened the memories of painful past traumas that were stored in every cell of my body. When I saw meetings set up with fellowship before the meeting, with an opening prayer, with the passing of an "offering" plate, with a message delivered, and with a closing prayer at the end, the similarities to the type services I had been exposed to while being abused were too much to bear. Mark assured me that my having a concept of the Power that might differ from his conception would not hinder our working the steps together effectively. He explained that the process of *really* working the steps would have none of those elements above that triggered part trauma and ongoing trauma. I am grateful that I found someone tolerant enough to allow me to have my own conception and who did not demand that I accept his. I learned later that he allowed that not only because of his charitable nature but also because the literature called for sponsors to be tolerant of alternative views.

The book that we have written is unlike any other I have read before or since because it is not expository. It does not *explain* to the readers certain information about the steps and how we worked them. Rather, the people who have read this book have testified that it is "experiential"—that they didn't just get more knowledge but that they actually had *an experience* with the events that are described herein. One said, "I was literally in the room with you two as Mark guided you. I felt your resistance. I experienced your surrender. I shared your awakening." The work that Mark completed with me did truly begin to unbind me and set me free. If you or someone you know is bound by addiction as I was, then I hope the same freedom might come to you or to your friend or relative through these pages. Love and Light, Floyd.

CHAPTER 5

"DO YOU HAVE A STORM

THAT NEEDS CALMING?"

By the time I met Mark, most of my life was one continuous series of storms: storms of the body, storms of the mind, storms of the emotions, and storms of the spirit. Bill W. said in his later talks that we have to attain all four levels of healing, all fours levels of sobriety, to get all the benefits available. He said that we alcoholics must go through four stages of healing—becoming spiritually sober, restoring our physical health, gaining mental well-being and addressing the emotional problems—in order to recover fully. To calm *all* the storms, therefore, Mark and I experienced the reality of the fact that all four areas must be treated. Thus we have arranged our book into sections that address the ways that we found treatment for each area of need that Bill W. identified.

In 1997 when we wrote what is now just "Part One" of this book, we could only have shared our experience in one of Bill W.'s four areas of sickness and one of his four levels of healing and sobriety. Today, with help from Mark and certain others, I have received what was required to calm all four of the sources of the storms in my life. A fellowship of people literally helped save my life; Mark H. unbound me from those things that were still restricting me; and the subsequent actions I took after working with Mark have taken me to a higher level of peace and serenity than I ever dreamed imaginable. All that came after finding the needed treatment and the subsequent healing that was needed for my body, my mind, and my emotions.

Do you have a storm raging inside you? How about two or three or four storms raging inside you, as identified by Bill W.? Have the storms led to the manifestation of other harmful dependencies or to continued problems...even after working the steps? Might you look at your life and see any similarity to mine when it was still ravaged by storms that I wanted to be freed of? If so, please read this book and see that if happiness, joy and freedom can come to a once miserable individual like Mark and to a once miserable individual like me, then it can come to anyone who is willing to take the action to complete a twelve-step journey to discover your Real SELF and is willing to take the subsequent action to treat all the parts that Bill W. said needed to be treated. May your reading of our book prove to be a freeing experience.

As explained, the book you hold will provide for you an actual experiencing of the process rather than a reading about the process. In Mark's clarity around the real problem and the founders' solution, Floyd would find one capable of guiding him away from the false and to the truth, thus initiating Floyd's shift from pain, to healing, to an awakening, and eventually into a state of permanent peace and an understanding of that which lies even beyond this relative existence. Let the experiencing of that process begin.

"WELL, MAYBE JUST ONE MORE

FOR THE ROAD"

"Hi. My name is Floyd and I'm an alcoholic."

"HI, FLOYD."

"Sorry I'm late. What's the topic? The First Step? When did I recognize that I was powerless over alcohol, that my life had become unmanageable? Well, let's go back to the days when my first marriage was ending.

"The three of us crashed through the front door screen and tumbled across my unmown lawn. My ex-wife rode me in a violent, clawing piggyback fashion as I clutched with one hand the elastic waistband on the rear of her mother's stretch pants and with my other hand the collar of the old woman's blouse. I was in the process of driving her face into the wire mesh screen of the door.

"The rear seam of her polyester double-knit slacks wedged into my ex-mother-in-law's dark abyss, causing what seemed to be entire bolts of material to disappear from view. My efforts caused the woman to stumble forward on her tiptoes with her arms extended, her hands flailing about in a bizarre kind of Dance of Hatred, a Ballet of War. Her stumbling, along with the drinks I'd consumed and with the added burden of 5'9" and 126 pounds of ex-wife on my back, caused me to lose my balance. *That* actually precipitated the fall that followed. See, it really wasn't *my* fault, the fact that they both ended up with injuries that afternoon. A study of the facts by any reasonable person would show that *they* caused the entire episode. In fact, you'll soon see that *I* was the victim in this incident. They hurt me much worse than I hurt them.

"The three of us, grasping, scratching, and fighting, tumbled lengthwise off the porch like three logs roped together. Where the sidewalk met the driveway, our rolling stopped as my head slammed into the pavement and I screamed out in pain. I released the old woman in order to clutch my head between my hands as I kicked in agony, lying on my back with my legs pumping into the air above me as if I were peddling away on an invisible bike. My ex-wife was up first and began indenting a space into my ribs with the toe of her shoe. The old woman was struggling to one knee, her corpulence having prevented the breaking of any of her cursed bones.

"Only thirty minutes before by phone, I had warned her to stay away during my arguments with her daughter. But no, she had to show up, to take sides, to suggest that I was pathological when angry and/or drunk. I lay on the edge of the driveway, bleeding severely from a forehead gash, a cut of the type that usually occurs only when two heavyweight boxers suffer a major head-butt. I touched my wound, and as I was studying the blood in my hands, my ex-wife was trying to hoist her mother from the drive. (*Where are all the cranes when you really need one?* I thought at the time.)

Gasping for air, arms intertwined, they limped each other to the old woman's car. They yelled something about 'If any…broken…police…jail…rest of your life!' As they drove away for their next-to-the-last-trip to the emergency room, I shook my pounding head to try to clear the combined fog of the alcohol and the blow I had received from the concrete. It was then that I finally noticed what sounded like the roaring whine of an electric weed-eater in my head.

"I thought, *Oh my gosh—that whining sound won't stop—I've really damaged something important this time!* Then I looked up and to my right to see my neighbor holding a piece of equipment in his arms—it really *was* a weed-eater I was hearing. He was frozen in amazement, having stopped his edging on my side of the drive between our houses. (He long ago had given up on waiting for me to edge or mow. He had also learned that letters from the homeowners' association were always tossed, unopened.) My face flushed in embarrassment at having lost a fight with two women in the presence of another man. I struggled to my feet and staggered just a little as I began to dust off my shirt and trousers. He closed his gaping mouth only long enough to swallow, after which his chin hung down again in amazement. His eyes were wide in disbelief and shock, and the expression on his face seemed to be begging for explanation, for some comment from me that would clarify what he still was not yet sure he had seen.

"To protect my sense of pride—I was a *very* proud man back then—and to use humor to relieve the tension of the situation in which I found myself, I said to him as I was turning to retreat inside: 'If we'd gone one-on-one in a *fair* fight, I guarantee you I could've kicked that old woman's ass.' My counterfeit laugh that followed the comment was not reciprocated.

"I walked inside to find the bottle I had left on the kitchen table. I needed a drink, and if you had to put up with the crap I put up with, you'd drink, too. Actually, maybe you did. Anyway, as I sat enjoying another stiff one on the rocks, it was for only a second that I flashed back to my last moments that day with Bill the Bartender when I had said to him: 'No more for me—cut me off right now,' followed many hours and many drinks later by, 'Well, maybe just one more for the road.'

"Evidencing some alcoholic tendencies herself, the ex had told me that she had abused her first husband and that I should knock the crap out of her if she ever struck me. Her alcoholic father echoed the same advice. Sounded like a good plan to me, so the Through-the-Screen-Door-Event would only set the stage for the final round in our years of fighting, the round in which I followed her suggestion, the round that moved me out of the house, the round that caused the loss of my bank accounts and all possessions except the one bed I owned when we married."

"So, Floyd," the newcomer at the table asked, "was that when you realized that you were powerless over alcohol and that your life had become unmanageable?"

"Hell, no. I drank for seventeen more years."

"MARK'S ANALYSIS OF FLOYD'S BEHAVIOR—STEP ONE"

"Delusion" is defined as "having a belief system that should be relinquished but that is held in spite of all evidence that it should be abandoned." That definition is especially applicable to alcoholics. If you look at the behaviors and the thoughts of the man as revealed in the previous story, you begin to appreciate the depth of the delusion that marks the alcoholic's life.

Alcoholism is a multi-level disease, and the manifestation of that disease is always observable through behaviors that the external world responds to with the question: "What is wrong with this person?" You see, the alcoholic man or woman suffers an illness that cripples the body, the mind, the emotions, and the spirit.

When the alcoholic takes a drink, his body breaks out in the phenomenon of craving for more alcohol, and he must drink to satisfy that craving, regardless of what he would like to do or what he should do. (*Floyd would learn later that the phenomenon of craving arises during the fourth stage of the breakdown of alcohol by the body. The metabolic process slows in real alcoholics but does not decrease in normal drinkers. When alcohol reaches the acetate form—which is broken down in the pancreas and the liver— the process slows since those organs function at a slower rate than in non-alcoholics, and it is the lingering presence of that acetate that triggers a craving for more. That physical phenomenon creates the allergy to alcohol in real alcoholics.*) That physical craving is coupled with a mind that tells the alcoholic time and time again that he can take that one drink and that something different will happen this time, something different from all of the negative things that happened every time before. He will think that he'll be able to control the amount that he will drink this time, even though years of experience have shown the alcoholic that such a thought is a lie.

Hence, we see the terrible dilemma that the alcoholic faces: first, he has a mind that lies to him over and over about all of his past experiences with alcohol as well as about the experience that he is about to undertake as he prepares to consume his next drink;

secondly, there exists no human power that can treat his alcoholism. His body is different and his mind is different. Then where, you ask, is the "hope" that is referred to in the literature?

Hope rests in the fact that the power of God, as the alcoholic comes to understand God, can bring about a change of mind. And the mind *must* change, for if the alcoholic's mind never told him again that he could drink normally, then he would never take the action of putting the next drink into his system. Then, neither he nor those around him would suffer all of the negative consequences.

Another key part of the disease is called the 'spiritual malady,' a condition that arises from the alcoholic having lived a life based on self-will ("playing God," if you will). A life run on the basis of self-will can be detected through recognition of the following symptoms: having trouble in personal relationships; having no ability to control one's emotional nature; being a prey to misery and depression; being full of fear; being unhappy; feeling useless; and being unable to make a satisfactory life, regardless of the alcoholic's external world.

The end result of this multi-tiered disease is observable in the preceding episode describing the altercation between the alcoholic, his wife, and her mother. We see in that one scene an exchange between three people that contains negative physical, emotional, verbal, and mental elements. Those four elements—which produced untold harm to all of the parties involved—arose after the alcoholic took the first drink, activated the phenomenon of craving, continued to drink to satisfy the craving, experienced the obsession of the mind, then moved into a thought-life based on self-will. We also see evidence of the alcoholic's inbred anger and rage over the fact that his self-will did not work. From that state of mind followed the fight, the verbal outbursts, and the insane thought-life that leads the alcoholic to say, "I could've kicked that old woman's ass" in a *fair* fight.

This event typifies the tragedy so often seen on a daily basis in the lives of alcoholics and all of the people whose lives they touch. And worst of all, in this case as in too many others, such behavior as his and such a thought-life as the one he displayed tragically continued for seventeen more years. It is small wonder, isn't it, that we are told that the alcoholic is beyond human help and must have divine help in order to recover?

"MARK GUIDES HIS PROTÉGÉ THROUGH STEP ONE"

"So, Floyd, we meet to begin working the steps together, and I find the story you've just repeated to me to be rather poignant. After having reflected on that account, there are some questions that you need to consider and answer. The first is: 'Are you willing to go to any length to recover from a hopeless state of body, mind, and spirit?' The second question is: 'Are you willing to take the necessary action to undergo a complete change of heart and mind'?"

"I'm totally beaten, Mark. What do I have to do?"

"Well, Floyd, what you have to do is have an *experience* with Step One of the program of recovery which I am willing to lead you through. That step asks you to admit that you are powerless over alcohol and that your life has become unmanageable."

"Heck, Mark, I know that already."

"Floyd, if there were any power in what you know—in your having knowledge of what is wrong with you—we wouldn't be having this discussion. You must *experience* your hopelessness to receive hope; you must *experience* your powerlessness to receive power; you must *experience* your insanity to be restored to sanity."

"Mark, that makes absolutely no sense."

"All your years of drinking and the subsequent consequences didn't make any sense either, but you did it all anyway, didn't you?"

Mark paused to allow Floyd all the time needed to relish and then drop the Go-to-Hell-look he was sending toward Mark. When Floyd gave it up, finally realizing that he would never win in a stare-down contest with Mark, the advisor moved on.

"Your only hope lies in the fact that you can *experience* the hopelessness, the powerlessness, and the insanity, so that's what we're going to begin doing right now. You see, the spiritual life, Floyd, is about your remembering what you already have in your heart and then unlearning everything in your programmed, conditioned mind that you have been taught by others. If there is not a complete change in your ideas, your thought-life, your emotions, your attitudes, and your beliefs, then you will never recover and you will be doomed to die an alcoholic death. If you allow your ego to lead you along a path other than the one I'm suggesting, so be it. But if you want to live on a spiritual basis, then we'll go through the steps of this recovery program together and you'll *experience* each one of them."

"I feel hopeless just hearing all of this."

"Well, you see, Floyd, the paradox about that is, the more hopeless you feel, the better it'll be."

"That's ridiculous."

Mark stared, silent. He had nothing to sell, nothing to force, nothing to push. He would have to see a sign of willingness from Floyd at each turn in order to continue. Finally, Floyd acquiesced.

"OK, maybe you're right. Nothing about all those years of drinking and the consequences made sense, either. Let's move on."

"Floyd, a lot of people make the experience of Step One a long and arduous road. We don't have to take that approach. You've already traveled a long and arduous road to reach this point in your life. Here's what we're going to do. We're going to travel together from that first drink you ever took, and we're going to go up to the very last drink that you took. And we're going to answer one simple question. That question is, 'Did you, at some point in your drinking career, lose control over the amount you drank, once you started drinking?' And by the way, Floyd, the answer to that question will be either 'Yes' or 'No,' based on your experience. Whether or not you have control over your drinking—once you start drinking—is not open to debate; either you had control or you didn't, once you took a drink. When we are through looking at your last drinking experience, you will be able to answer the question, 'Did that happen to me?' If it did, then you are powerless over alcohol, once alcohol enters your body. Now, Floyd, is that simple enough for your complex mind?"

"You don't have to be a jerk about it, Mark." Floyd paused, and

those steely eyes of Mark's penetrated deeply. Finally, Floyd acquiesced again: "Yeah, that's simple enough."

My, Floyd…you are *so* sensitive—a serious handicap that I
hope you'll outgrow. You seem to be rather uptight. Let me ask
you this, Floyd. Do you know what it means to 'be still'?"

"Sure—it means 'don't move'."

"We'll see if that's what it means to you after we go through
the work together. For now, the second thing we'll do, Floyd, is
we'll look at your thought-life around alcohol *when you were sober*.
We'll look at your *sober* experience, when you had no alcohol in
your body, and we'll look for certain states-of-mind that took you
back to the first drink. Do you know what 'sober' means, Floyd?"

"Of course. It means, 'not drunk'."

"We'll also see if that is your understanding by the time we
complete our work together. For now, let's talk about those states-
of-mind."

"What are 'states-of-mind'?"

"I refer to thoughts you did or did not have concerning drinking. For example, based on your experience, did you lose the ability to choose whether you drank or not? Did you always have a
mental defense against the first drink, finding yourself able to say
'No' when the thought crossed your mind to take a drink? Did
that mental defense work for you every time? Did the knowledge
of what you did in the past while drinking help stop you from taking a drink again at a later time? Do you have the power to think
through the consequences of taking a drink? Have you ever 'suddenly thought that it would be OK to take a drink'? Have you ever
found yourself drinking and found that you had experienced a
strange mental blank spot before taking the first drink? You see,
Floyd, if—when you were sober—any of those states-of-mind were
experienced, then you have already experienced the hopelessness
of alcoholism. And you experienced those thoughts while you were
at your best, *sober*!

Floyd sat quietly, shocked into silence as he received at least
a slim flicker of truth by way of Mark's questions. He saw that
every time he'd gotten drunk, he had first begun to move to the

intoxicated state from a state of sobriety, thinking that *things would be different this time.*

Mark continued, "You've always thought that when it came to alcohol that you could take it or leave it, but you're going to find out that you have a body that can't take it and a mind that can't leave it alone. Eventually, your obsessive mind will take you into a strange mental blank spot where all of your self-knowledge and all of your willpower are unavailable to you. In fact, isn't that your experience already, Floyd?"

"Before I answer, let me make sure I understand this. You're telling me that at my very best, with all of the reasons for never taking a drink at my command, I will drink again...if I have an alcoholic mind?"

"Well, Floyd, look at your own experience. Isn't that what you've been doing?"

Floyd sat in the silence again, unwilling at first to concede the point. Finally, he admitted, "I guess it is. So you're telling me that the obsession of my mind makes me drink against my will—in other words, against all my willpower—yet my body allergy makes me want to drink even when it hurts me so much when I do? That leaves me with the hopeless feeling I'm getting now that I can't change my body's allergy."

"Floyd, you're getting smarter. That allergy will never leave. It will only get worse as your organs age."

"So what about this 'unmanageable' stuff? I've managed to do pretty well in a lot of areas in my life, Mark. I'd like to get a little credit for that."

"I'll bet you would, Floyd; in fact, I'd bet you would like to get *a lot of* credit for that, but for now, there are other things we're going to consider."

A pout crossed Floyd's face. Mark took a moment to try to assign an age to the part inside Floyd that was inspiring that. *Somewhere around twelve, I'd guess.*

Finally, Mark went on. "The first need right now is to understand that unmanageability is not a condition that exists outside of you. It's a condition that exists *inside* yourself. Once inside you, it will then eventually manifest itself externally. It's a state-of-mind, a state of body, an emotional state, and a state of spiritual sickness in which all four of those parts are 'dis-eased,' not at ease. Its symptoms are that you have trouble in your personal relationships, including, most importantly, the one that you have with yourself; that you can't control your emotional nature; that you are a prey to misery and depression; that you can't make a life that is satisfying to you; that you're full of fear; that you're unhappy; and that you can't seem to be of real help to other people. This condition begins to manifest itself *externally* in your life in those eight areas, Floyd, because the condition exists first *inside* you."

Floyd again remained quiet, reviewing the cataloguing of the eight traits of untreated alcoholism that Mark had just enumerated. Ultimately, Floyd conceded, "Mark, I guess *some* of those might apply to my life. There have been times when I had money, lots of it; times when I had family and a job and everything else, but I still experienced those symptoms. What the heck's wrong with me, Mark?"

"Well, Floyd, we do have a name for the condition that results in these symptoms. It's called the 'spiritual malady.' It comes from attempting to live your life based on self-will—from playing God, if you will—with everybody and everything in your life. And the terrible dilemma that you face, Floyd, is that there's nothing *you* can do about your self-will. Your self-will cannot eliminate your self-will. Only God as you'll conceive of that Power can treat this spiritual malady. When the spiritual malady is overcome, your thought-life will change and you might begin to seek help for your grave emotional and mental issues and you might stop doing harmful things to your body. You might even start exercising some day! Ha. Now, Floyd, do you see why you're 100% hopeless, apart from receiving this help for your spirit, if you're a *real alcoholic*?"

After consideration, Floyd admitted, "I can't argue that. What can we do?"

"We can move on to Step Two, Floyd."

Chapter 7—Step Two

"Driving B. J. Crazy"

Taking a seat at the table of a meeting already in progress, the chairperson said, "Hello, Floyd. Glad you could make the meeting, but it starts at 10:00, not 10:20."

"Sorry I'm late, but I spilled hot coffee on my lap in the car, so I stopped to call a lawyer in the fellowship to tell him 'I think we have a case!'"

"And did he agree?"

"Actually, he said: 'You *are* a case—now wipe off your car seat and go to a meeting.' So here I am."

"Well, it seems your timing is perfect because we're talking about alcoholic insanity."

Laughter exploded forth from those already seated. The look Floyd gave the chairperson could have killed, had Floyd's face been a weapon. The chair continued, "Tommy, here, being relatively new, is having a little trouble accepting the fact that some of his behaviors might have been a little insane. Would you like to share—maybe talk about that comeback you made up for your first wife's accusations that you were crazy?"

"Sure, be glad to. My name is Floyd, and I'm an alcoholic."

"HI, FLOYD."

"I remember the first time I was able to use the line. I was ready and waiting for her to attack me with those two words. I didn't have to wait long."

"You're nuts!" she yelled.

"'*What about 'em?*' I yelled back. I had to bite my gum to keep from laughing out loud, I was so proud! I delighted in her speechlessness and that look of wonder that crossed her face, trying at first to figure out the meaning, then the realization; then the disgust; then the look—the one that said, 'My gosh . . . I've married a 12-year old.' Then she walked away. *Victory! I had the final word*, I thought.

"Then she stuck her head back into the room, and the drinks I had consumed make her exact words difficult to remember today but they were something like, 'You and your precious dog B.J. are both insane. I'm sick of both of you staggering around this house drunk, and I want you both out of here.'

"Now, of all her accusations, the two that bugged me the most were suggesting, first, that *I* had a problem with alcohol, and secondly, that B.J. had *any* kind of problem. The truth is, on many occasions she had caught us both DWI ('Drinking While Intoxicated'), but I wasn't about to admit it.

"I said, 'B.J. is a million times more faithful to me than your cold-blooded heart has ever allowed you to be, so shut your mouth about B.J.!'

"I hate both of you," she shouted. "You nearly killed my mother throwing her off the porch and now you've trained B.J. to attack her and latch onto her neck. I want y'all out of here." A sinister smile crossed my face as I pictured my dog's teeth attached to the neck of the old woman.

"I answered, 'I never trained B.J. to bite anybody. He naturally attacks those that he thinks are a threat to him or to me. I wish *you'd* defend me as well against those who are always attacking me.'

"Later, my psychologist would say that I had substituted B.J. for all my lost friends. He became my drinking partner—half-collie, half-beagle, all-male. And he was quite normal...for a while. Later, my ex-wife would claim *he* needed therapy from a pet psychologist. I asked, 'How can I afford therapy for my dog when I'm buying a hundred pairs of shoes per year for you?'

"'Maybe you can find a discounted group rate for the both of you,' she said. (I hadn't realized at that point that even driving down the road alone I was in group therapy.) But her comment reminded me why I hated her guts. She hated me, too, but I can't remember why. On the other hand, we must have loved each other or we couldn't have gotten as upset during our fights as we got. I might still be a little confused in that area.

"Anyway, looking back objectively, my influence on B.J. may have had a slightly negative effect on him. I had trained him exactly. When I spoke, 'Heel!' he would heel. When I spoke, 'Lie down!' he would lie down. When I gave the signal to attack, he would attack. Any Marine D.I. would have envied the strict regimen and subsequent results of my canine-training skills. I was obsessive; I was dogmatic; I was doggone proud.

"As the dog's personality distorted, I tried to talk some sense into him. My ex-wife said that was the problem to begin with. I hated her for that, too. She had always resented the fact that I wouldn't tell her what the letters 'B' and 'J' stood for. Her insecure mind worked up all sorts of combinations and possibilities, but the truth was that I had named the dog for my alcoholic cousin—a man I figured was a picture of what a *real alcoholic* looked like. He couldn't drink socially, as I could. He couldn't quit if he wanted to, as I could. He couldn't keep a job, as I sometimes could.

"In the meantime, as B.J. drank more and more of what I poured regularly into his bowl, his mental condition worsened; nevertheless, we drew closer for some reason. He seemed to love what I loved; he seemed to hate what I hated. We both hated a lot. We were like brothers in other ways, too. We both spent a lot of time barking at people; we both chased the opposite sex; we both relieved ourselves where we pleased, when we pleased. He could handle his beer, but I eventually cut him off the hard stuff. He'd pass out and I'd have no company. The trick he did that I liked best, though, involved the old woman.

"My ex-wife would invite her over either for our fights or our food. I really resented the nights she ate our food—like she needed to eat anyone's food. My favorite trick that B.J. pulled would occur when the old woman sat in my chair. Yeah, my ex-wife bought it since she made most of the money, but I had legitimately staked out a claim on it so it was mine.

"I resented the old woman being in my chair. Now B.J.'s legs were like springs. From a flat-footed position behind the chair, with no running start, he could jump to the thick back of the leather, pub-type chair. From there, it was only a short trip for his jaws to lock onto the old woman's neck. All that was required for the process to begin was a slight nod of my head after he had moved into attack position. I always wondered why the old woman fell for this one so many times. It's like *she* was the insane one, doing the same thing over and over and expecting a different result. Did she really think the next time would be different? Did she really think we'd let her get away with insulting me like that, by sitting in my chair?

"I would love to see B.J. moving into position, hunched down low, moving slowly toward her in the way that a cat approaches a mouse, sneaking stealthily over to his spot of attack behind my chair. He looked at me time and again as he approached the old woman. My smile was his license to proceed. Now he was in posi- tion, stooping to launch himself. He froze and looked for my sig- nal, and as soon as I nodded, he sprang! Now he was atop the chair, then leaning over the back of the chair with a leg on her shoulder, growling louder than a bear protecting her cubs. His jaws had her throat, again! I gave him a license, alright—a license to kill.

"Then she was pulling forward in the chair, like one of those bulls thcy used to stake out in pits in England in the old days when they'd let the bulldogs cling to the sides of the bulls. The bulls twisted in pain, trying to throw off the attack dogs. That was the picture before me. I was on both knees, the top of my head forward with my forehead on the carpet, pounding my fist into the floor, howling in my laughter, screaming even louder than the old woman. I wish I'd had a VCR camera back then. Now here comes my ex- wife, running into the living area from the kitchen and kicking at B.J. the way she often kicked me when I was down. By now the old woman had joined me on the floor on both her knees, B.J. still hanging on for dear life, pulling, as if trying to drag her out of the house, just the way I'd shown him once before at the screen door.

Usually by this point, I was deprived of enjoying the rest of the scene since those hoses that stop just under the knee would start showing. A gag-reflex would usually send my head spinning away from the scene about then. I was sensitive, for a man, and my stomach couldn't take too much of certain disgusting sights.

"That was only one of the many instances when that dog and I teamed up to create some excitement, like the time B.J. barked at the gas meter reader from the dog's secured place behind our cyclone fence. The reader sprayed B.J. with mace in spite of the fact that he was behind the fence, thereby provoking me to attack the gas company employee. He ended up lying in the same spot on our driveway where I had been bleeding years before. My ex-wife claims my attack of the meter reader—to defend B.J.—was our most memorable fiasco because the gas company pulled our meter and we were going to have to buy all new electric stuff: a new electric clothes dryer, electric water heater, electric range and oven, and an electric heating system for the house. My ex-wife ended up getting the meter reinstalled after she paid all the fines and settlements, along with a huge deposit, so I reminded her that she had made a big deal out of nothing. I hate when people make a big deal out of nothing. Personally, I thought the veterinarian deal was our moment of greatest triumph. It came about two years after the Famous Fight at the Screen Door.

"I had dropped B.J. off at the animal clinic for some shots and a cut, shampoo and blow dry. The receptionist estimated four hours, but by the time I had driven home, the phone was already ringing with a call from their office. I was impressed that they were going to be keeping me informed of B.J.'s progress during the procedure. Obviously, they had seen how attached to him I was.

"Instead, when the vet got on the line, he yelled: 'Your friggin' dog has bitten two of us. This pest is certifiably insane and needs to be put to sleep for the common good. If he proves not to be rabid after observation, we will be glad to perform euthanasia on him without charge.' Then he slammed the phone down in my ear. I was enraged. I was furious. And I was excited. I found rage stimulating in those days. It got my juices flowing. I was as addicted to chaos as I was to the booze, almost. I needed to feel that adrenaline flow.

"I salivated at the prospect of crying 'Havoc' and 'letting slip the dogs of war' as I headed to that office to seek my revenge. I imagined my fist re-shaping the face of that doctor as it might if it were striking a huge ball of clay, smashing in the visage so badly that it stayed in that newly-molded shape forever. I dreamed that every morning as long as he lived, that vet would walk into the bathroom, look into the mirror, see the impression of my fist reflected from his concave face, and review each day the price to be pay for his rudeness.

"Sometimes for months afterwards I fantasized about spraying the entire office with machinegun fire and then surveying the destruction in the same way that Audie Murphy used to do in his WWII flicks. I would have his look on my face, the one he had as he stepped over dead bodies on the battlefield, the one that seemed to say, 'Death is such a terrible thing—I wish it were not necessary, but I know in my heart that having done this deed makes the world a better place, so it was justified.'

"I screamed as I raced in and out of traffic on the way to that office, but then streets were always a battleground to me. *Only the bold and the strong survive*, I surmised. If I didn't drive like a maniac among all the stupid people allowed on the road, I would never get anywhere. Actually, I felt I deserved an open road ahead of me. I should have been able to put DYOLF on the front of my car so all could look into their mirrors and know to pull over and make way.

"'That jerk insults my flesh and blood and then uses the worst possible telephone etiquette to boot!' I screamed. Fortunately for him, he was not in the office when I arrived. I stormed into the rear section, aides and assistants yelling for me to stop. I found his cage and released B.J. from his incarceration. I hitched a leash to his collar to get him out of there before the police arrived, but his attraction to the dog in the next cage nearly overrode my efforts to escape. Neither he nor I ever thought straight when it came to the opposite sex. As I pulled, his two foremost legs locked into a position straight to his front as he tried to impede my pulling him across the tile. His rear slid across the slick, cold tiles of the floor.

"He was near the center of the long hallway when I noticed that all of the screaming and excitement had caused him to start to defecate. My dragging him along succeeded in spreading his muddle over half the length of that hall and then down the next corridor. He continued his mess-making as we crossed the formerly white tiles of the receiving area. He then jumped to all fours to snap at several other animals in the room as we headed for the door.

"By now, the receptionist was quiet—OK, actually *speechless*—but she really came to life when I paused just long enough for B. J.'s final act of revenge. He had pulled the leash tight as he bolted ahead to smell the straw basket that held a silk fichus tree near the exit. No one in the office had any doubts about his intentions, and I paused just long enough for my lingering B.J. to make a territorial mark upon the basket. It was official: we *owned* that office. I was in total control. The receptionist looked faint; a child laughed and pointed out the event to his startled mom. I, in turn, allowed them all to see the cynical, twisted smile on my face that always came in such gloating moments of, in my mind, total triumph. Victory, again! I winked at the kid as I walked through the door, and he blinked both eyes back at me, squishing up his whole face in the process. Then he opened his eyes and smiled. I had made another friend. He became one more of the many people who liked me. At least I think they liked me.

"I tasted victory everywhere I went, for everywhere I went there was a battle to be fought, a battle to be won by me. The look I gave to all people screamed out the message 'Take that!'

"Leaving the office and driving home with B.J. barking at all the idiots on the road (OK...actually with *both* of us barking at all the idiots on the road) I could now rest, the score having been evened. In my mind, the Great Tennis Referee of the Games of Life that I played had just declared, 'Advantage . . . Floyd!'" (B.J. was, you see, not the only one leaving behind a trail of blood, sweat, tears, and a bunch of crap for others to clean up.)

"So, Floyd, was that when you realized that you needed to be restored to sanity?"

"Heck, no. I drank for fifteen more years!"

"MARK'S ANALYSIS OF FLOYD'S BEHAVIOR—STEP TWO"

The alcoholic dilemma continues for Floyd and others like him. An alcoholic is like a tornado roaring through the lives of others, leaving a trail of undeserved tears, wrecked cars, broken homes and broken hearts in a destructive path…all the while saying, "Nothing's really wrong here. If only 'they' would change or understand me or appreciate me, everything would be all right."

In the Second Step, Floyd and all alcoholics must embrace the idea that they can come to believe—that they can find a Power greater than themselves that will restore them to sanity. As shown in the story, Floyd's actions, thoughts and emotions are not those of a sane individual. A realization of "Floyd's truth by Floyd" must be recognized before he will become open-minded about the idea of a God, in whatever way he comes to conceive of God, that can restore Floyd to sanity.

Floyd must have a deep experience with the hopelessness of his mind, body, emotions, and spirit in Step One before he will become open-minded about seeking a God of his understanding in Step Two. It is only through utter desperation that the alcoholic reaches a position of surrender, a position in which the alcoholic can no longer delude himself that his self-will, his way, is working; hence, we then see the truth of the statement, "The more hopeless the alcoholic feels, the better," for it is then that he will be willing to follow suggestions.

It is in this step that Floyd will face his doubts and his prejudices, that is, his preconceived thoughts and opinions about God. (Because of circumstances of abuse in his past and in his present, he showed up on my doorstep with certain notions that would surprise no one.) And if alcohol—which is always, ultimately, the Teacher—has beaten him into a state in which he can be *open-minded* about having a new experience with God and not just having certain beliefs about God, then Floyd has an opportunity to bring about conscious contact with a God of his own, *new* conception. Then he will also bring about conscious contact with love and sanity. By the way, hard drinkers and moderate drinkers do not have to have the experiences we are discussing because they have power over alcohol. The *real alcoholic* does not, and his course of action (and consequently, his experience in seeking God) must be different.

"MARK GUIDES HIS PROTÉGÉ THROUGH STEP TWO"

"So here we are again, Floyd, and it's time for you to make another decision. You have to decide now if you want to *experience* Step Two."

"Explain."

"Floyd, in this step, we will come to believe that a Power greater than ourselves can restore us to sanity." *Dharma, Spiritual law, God's will, etc*

Floyd grimaced. This time, Mark decided to ignore the look and move on, for he knew what he faced and he knew what had to be accomplished to help Floyd.

"No alcoholic will take this step, Floyd, until he has experienced his insanity. As a matter of fact, Floyd, I feel sorry for people who have never experienced insanity, because they don't really know what sanity feels like or looks like. We do. Aren't we lucky?"

"There you go again, Mark, saying things that don't make sense. Some of the things that you've said in the past I've come to understand, but I don't get that one."

"Floyd, to know and experience God, you must be out of your mind—and you certainly meet that criterion. Ha!"

Floyd opened his mouth to speak, but he didn't.

"Do you understand what I mean when I say that you must be out of your mind to know and experience God?"

"No, but I know what the phrase 'being restored to sanity' implies, and I've got to tell you that I don't like the implication even a little bit."

"So, you don't like the implication of a statement. Well let me ask this. How do you like the life you're leading? How do you like the way you feel?"

Again, were Floyd's face a weapon, Mark would not be alive today. And again, Mark knew it was time to confront. Resistance was increasing.

"Floyd, you may as well understand this before we go any further. I speak truth, and with guys like you, the truth will set you free but it's gonna really piss you off first. So do you think that sensitivity we talked about earlier can handle the truth required for you to be free?"

Floyd had to think about that. He *actually* had to think about whether he wanted truth and freedom as opposed to lies and mental and emotional imprisonment. Mark watched as the gears turned, having seen such insanity for years among many whom he has guided through the steps. It never failed to amaze and ultimately amuse to see people having to contemplate before being able to answer that question.

"Of course I want the truth," Floyd lied without knowing it. That was enough, though, for Mark to continue.

"What I mean when I say that you must be out of your mind to know and experience God is that the God of your understanding will be known and experienced, Floyd, with a part of your being that has always been there but has been—in your case—a part that you have been asleep to. In fact, Floyd, believe it or not, you have been asleep most of your life. You have gone through life unaware, unconscious, and asleep—thinking all the time that you were awake. When you look back at the story of you and B.J., can't you get some idea of what I mean?"

"I guess I really wasn't totally aware of how wrong some of that stuff was that we did, how crazy *some* of it was. Now that you mention it, I guess it was like I went into some unconscious state. I'd get so mad that I'd go off into some zone."

"Actually, you just 'went off,' on everyone, but let's talk about God."

"That's another thing, Mark. I've suffered abuse at the hands of a lot of so-called 'godly' or 'religious' people in my life. I'm having trouble with that part."

"Then we'll pause before we talk about God anymore. I'm surprised that you haven't come up with a conception that you can be comfortable with. For gosh sakes, even your dog B.J. has a concept of God."

The Floyd who took himself to be so wise suddenly had a very dumb look on his face. The silence inspired by Mark's comment allowed him to continue uninterrupted for a change.

"Let me ask you two questions: first, what concept of God do you think your dog B.J. might have? And secondly, where do you imagine that concept came from?"

After some moments taken to absorb what Mark might be talking about, Floyd was able to answer. "Well, I guess that his concept of 'God,' so to speak, would have been *me*. I guess to him *I* was God since I fed him and took care of all his needs."

"Now we're getting somewhere, Floyd. And where did that concept come from?"

"Well, I guess it would have been formed from his interactions with me. I provided for him. I took care of him. So I modeled for him what a God or protector or whatever we call it might look like."

"Good answer, Floyd!" So my next question is, where did you get *your* concept of God—the one that you passed on down the line to B.J.? Think about this before answering, Floyd. You experienced in Step One the fact that no human power can restore you to sanity, sanity really just being 'a change of heart and a change of mind.'

"Hummm. I like that idea of sanity a little better than what I pictured earlier."

"Yeah—I thought you might. So if B. J.'s concept of God came from the relationship that he had with you and from the ideas that you presented him, then your concept must have come from the relationship you had with your father and from the ideas that you were presented with as a child. Doesn't that make sense?"

"Wow! I can see that, Mark, how that happens. And the God-like authority in my life was often caring but could also be punishing and judgmental. There was a 'hug-slug element' to our relationship."

"So you formulated a concept of a God who could be relied

on some times but who at other times was not there for you or was punishing you if he was there. No wonder you're having trouble with this concept. Floyd, here's something you must understand in order to progress: I see God as a creator. Your father was your creator; therefore, you are a creator, too. This is vital, Floyd. Get a grip on this notion. Can you realize that God, as you understand God or don't understand God, is really just a concept that you created? Doesn't that follow?"

"I never thought of it like that, Mark, but it makes sense. The concept I have of God is the concept I created, and I created it based on my experience with the authority figures I knew."

"In order for you to know and to experience God, I want you to give me—to create with me, if you will—a concept of God that will work for you. Come up with a concept of a God that you would want to know personally...a Power that you could be comfortable around. Right now—tell me what that Power would be like."

"Well, that Power would be loving and forgiving. That Power would give wise guidance and be protective."

"Then so be it, Floyd. All you have to do now is start experiencing *that* concept. And then guess what, Floyd—the new concept that you have created to replace the old concept that you created will manifest itself."

Mark's words—combined with the excitement of such a possibility—shocked Floyd once again into a state of silence, much to Mark's delight. That allowed Mark to say, "Upon this simple cornerstone, Floyd, you can then begin to effect conscious contact with the God of your new understanding. So is it OK with you if I continue now that we have reached that new perception?"

"Rock and roll, Bro."

"Step Two, Floyd, is about three things: first, it's about a willingness to believe in a Power greater than yourself; next, it's about coming up with a concept of God that is comfortable to you; and, finally, it's about making a choice about that Power. And here is the choice, Floyd: you are faced with a self-imposed crisis which has resulted in a lack of power, in insanity, and in hopelessness. So are you willing to make this choice: that the God of your new understanding is everything in your life, just as B.J. accepts unquestioningly that you are everything in his life?"

"Seeing what I saw in Step One, and what I'm seeing now, I don't guess I really have any other choice, do I?"

"Good, Floyd. Then the next thing to understand is that the only place that you will come to know and experience God is deep down inside yourself, not outside yourself. You are blocked from knowing that which sustains you because of your self-will, Floyd. You have been playing God all of your life. Why would you seek power if you think you *are* the power? If you're willing to give up that belief system, and if you're willing to search fearlessly within yourself, the God of that conception you just came up with will be revealed. Are you willing to seek that Power through this course of action?"

"I see now that alcohol is what I've been worshipping, so what have I got to lose?"

"Your unmanageable life and your absolute insanity, Floyd."

Floyd's comment will be censored from the text, but Mark's laughter showed how little such vile comments affect him.

"IF YOU START SOMETHING, FINISH IT!"

"We're talking about Step Three today—making a decision to turn our will and our lives over to the care of God as we understood him. Who would like to share?"

"Yeah, my name's Floyd, and I'm an alcoholic."

"HI, FLOYD!"

"Mark and I have talked some about my having trouble with 'the God part,' and he recently helped me get past that hurdle. We had to go way back, all the way to the beginning, to find the source of the beliefs I fostered that made it difficult for me to turn my life over to anybody, even a Higher Power. I was in the third grade and dad and I were having a talk at the end of one night:

"OK, Floyd—have you got your clothes laid out for school?"

"Yes sir."

"Did you do all of your homework?"

"Yes sir."

"Now, about this fighting at school. Do you remember what I told you about fighting, what I learned about life in WWII?"

"Yes, sir: 'Don't start a fight, but if someone else starts a fight, I finish it'."

"All right. Get to sleep."

"Yes sir."

[8 hours later]

"Floyd, get up. Get off to school."

"Yes sir."

[10 hours later]

"5 A's and a 'B' in math. What's the problem in math?"

"I don't know, sir."

"Did you bring your math book home to do some extra work?"

"No, sir. I forgot."

"Well maybe this belt will help you remember."

[Afterwards]

"Stop crying—big boys don't cry. You want to cry, I'll give you something to cry about. If you do something, do it right. There's no such thing as 'can't.' Don't be a quitter; if you start something, finish it. Just make up your mind to do it and then do it. It's a dog-eat-dog world out there, and if you aren't prepared for the fight, you're gonna lose. Be the best at whatever you do. I'm not gonna feed you all your life, so you're gonna be on your own, and the way you're going, you're gonna starve."

[Eleven year later, during an all-night study session with two fellow students preparing for a college philosophy exam]

"Hey, Floyd. What do you think about the prof's idea that we base our conceptions of God on the way we saw our own dominant parent?"

"I don't know."

"Well, what do you think God is like?"

"I think He's harsh, mean, unpredictable, and judgmental. He keeps up with our performance and is very critical of us when we don't perform perfectly. I think He's dogmatic and punitive, but when He punishes us, He says he does it because He loves us."

"What about people who have faith in Him, who surrender to Him?"

Floyd shot his best Go-to-Hell-look across the room. The third student present asked, "Why do you say 'He?' Why does God have to be a male?"

"Because He's a male, you idiot," Floyd answered. Then to the other, "For one thing, I'm not sure He cares about anybody. The way I've lived, He's probably already made up His mind to send me to hell forever, so my only chance at experiencing any enjoyment is by doing what I want in this life. As far as giving up or surrendering, as far as admitting that there's something I can't do, my response is…there's no such thing as 'can't.' I surrender to no one. If you start something with me, I'll finish it. It's just like Caesar told his wife in the play written by Shakespeare: 'Cowards die many times before their death; the valiant never taste of death but once'."

"Floyd, there's one thing you can't do. You can't respond to a question with only a 'Yes' or a 'No' answer! By the way, why are you drinking on the night before this big test?"

"Hey, I just told you: If I start something, I finish it. I started this bottle, so I'm gonna finish it!"

"MARK'S ANALYSIS OF FLOYD'S BEHAVIOR—STEP THREE"

In Step One, Floyd discovered his multi-part problem: one, he's powerless over alcohol, and two, he needs to be restored to sanity. He discovered also that he is insane around alcohol, in his thought-life, and in his emotions. Furthermore, he learned that he's hopeless. The paradox is that, once an alcoholic like Floyd *experiences* these three states of consciousness, there is suddenly great hope for him.

It is from powerlessness that power shows up for the person who sees that he really has no power or control and then begins the search for needed power. It is from an awareness of insanity that sanity begins to show up as he searches for a different way of thinking. And it is from hopelessness that hope begins to manifest as a person being restored to sanity also begins to search for ways to solve seemingly hopeless circumstances. Floyd, like all *real alcoholics*, had to realize that some Power must show up in his life to restore him to sanity.

In Step Two, he was faced with his beliefs and prejudices about God. He had to fearlessly face them and be willing to lay them aside. And we are not talking about his merely developing a belief in God. Having faced his beliefs and prejudices—and having set them aside—the alcoholic must then come up with a God that is

meaningful, that is personal, that will become revealed to an alcoholic, and that will be a constructive Power. I had to be willing to
allow him to come up with a God of his own conception so that
we could move forward. The only requirement for moving on is that
Floyd make a choice that his God—the God of his new understanding—will be Everything to him. Having done that, the only
thing left for the alcoholic to do is to be willing to seek conscious
contact with the God within. The promise is that the Power will
become revealed if we are willing to seek.

Now, the alcoholic must face three ideas, and he must be thor- *[here is the hard part]*
oughly convinced of their validity: the first is that he really is an alcoholic and that his life is unmanageable; next, that no human power
can restore him to sanity; and, last, that God can restore him to sanity—and will—if the alcoholic is willing to seek the Power.

Having arrived at this point, the drunk must then make a decision to turn his will and his life over to God. The requirement to
make this decision and to follow through with action is based upon
the alcoholic's experiencing the truth of the fact that any life run
on self-will will not work. He must admit that, at his very best, he *[seeing]*
creates confusion in his life and the lives of others. The alcoholic *[himself]*
must recognize that it is from this state of consciousness (or actu- *[as separate.]*
ally a lack of consciousness) that his self-will is running riot, that
he is playing God, and that he is creating the very state-of-mind that
keeps taking him back to the drink time and time again.

You see, a life run on self-will will not work in our universe
because our universe—with all of its interconnectedness—can run
smoothly only when all of its parts are in harmony with all of its
other parts, when all of its parts are at ease with all of its other parts.
Ultimately, in fact, things run the smoothest when there is no perception of separate "parts" but instead a Pure Consciousness of
the Connectedness or, more accurately, the Oneness. Thus, a life
run on self-will—absorbed with living and experiencing the world
while concerned only with self—is naturally going to create "dis-
ease." One can see, then, why the alcoholic is restless, irritable,
and discontented; unfortunately, from this state-of-mind, the only
treatment the alcoholic can recall that he thinks will ease his "dis-

Here is the part that I'm not sure d. long

ease" is a drink. So he takes a drink. That drink activates the phenomenon of craving and from that point, there is no stopping...for
the *real alcoholic*.

Self-will must die if the alcoholic is to live. Either the selfishness must die or the alcoholic will live miserably and die early. The
terrible dilemma that the alcoholic finds himself in at this stage of
working the steps is that he can do nothing of his own power to
eliminate his selfishness, his self-will. He must have God's help, and
to get God's help, he must decide to quit playing God. This decision can only be reached by experiencing the great fact that his
playing God has not worked in the past, cannot work now, and
will not work in the future.

At this point, we make our Third Step decision, which is to turn
our will and life over to the care of God as we now conceive of that
Power. In making that decision, we proclaim that, from this day on,
God will be the Director of our lives; that God will be the Principal
in our lives; that God will be the Father in our lives. This becomes
the Third Step decision, a decision that must be followed by even
more action.

"MARK GUIDES HIS PROTÉGÉ THROUGH STEP THREE"

"Well, Floyd, here we sit again, one alcoholic with another
alcoholic, sharing experience, strength, and hope. You remember
why we're meeting today, don't you?"

"Yeah. Today's the day that I'll make my Third Step decision
to seek conscious contact with the God of my understanding
because of my truth experienced in Step One and the commence-
ment of knowing God outside of my mind in Step Two. I want to
tell you something before we go on."

"Man, I like hearing what you just said. Go ahead."

"Having done what you told me—coming up with a new concept of the power—I've started to understand other things you
said. I understand that the power I believe in will manifest through
my new concept. I used to think of a male God who was harsh,
mean, unpredictable, and judgmental—that's how I saw a God
showing up in my life. You were so right: I had created a God

rooted in the perceptions formed during my childhood experiences. That God had to be of a male gender and was a God I could never please or get approval from—regardless of what I accomplished and regardless of what I did. At least, that was my perception. The Power I'm beginning to sense now is the power of Love, Forgiveness, Sane Guidance, and Constructive Creation. I'm free to create that new understanding that is going to make my recovery possible, I believe. I never understood this before. My life has already begun to change since you helped me create a new concept of a Higher Power and since I have started to tap into that Power. What I don't understand is why I'm making this thing you call a 'Third Step decision'."

"Floyd, you've started to undergo a change of heart and mind, haven't you? I hear it in what you just said."

"Yeah, I guess I have. And I don't completely understand that either, but you said I would experience the truth and know the truth. You said that words would not be necessary for me to comprehend my Real *SELF* or my Spirit or True Consciousness—that I'll feel something more like a 'knowing.' I think that's happening."

"Floyd, that's what is called the 'knowing and experiencing of God' as you understand the Power. Now in this decision that you're going to make, it's important to understand why you're making it, so we're definitely going to review. There are some requirements you must meet before making the decision. First, are you convinced that your life run on your self-will doesn't work?"

"You've shown me that."

"OK. Then do you realize that, at your best, you still have trouble in personal relationships?"

"Admittedly."

"And do you see that the relationship you are having the most trouble with is the one with yourself since all your other troubles are coming from that one?"

"I can't argue that."

"Now, Floyd, I know a simple 'Yes' or 'No' answer is difficult for you, but that's all the answer I want to the following questions.

Can you give me a simple 'Yes' or 'No' answer?"

"Well, I would think that would depend on...."

"Floyd! Stop! 'Yes'...or 'No!' No more! Now listen. Do you realize that you can't control your emotional nature, that is, you react and overreact too easily?"

After a long pause in which Floyd would truly have loved to explain to Mark all the different aspects of that question that needed to be addressed, and after getting angry that Mark would not let him explain, he finally realized that even *that* series of thoughts provided a perfect example of his overreacting. So he conceded, "Yes," but he still despised one-word answers.

"Do you realize that you are a prey to misery and depression, especially when life doesn't go the way you want it to go?"

"Yesssss," he said sarcastically, dragging out the answer so it at least didn't *seem* like one word. Mark totally ignored the childishness, understanding the subconscious roots that were still driving much of Floyd's behavior.

"Do you realize that you can't make a living, meaning that you cannot create on your own power a life that is satisfactory and that brings you peace and ease?"

"Yes."

"Do you realize that you are full of fear and that when self-will is running the show and life doesn't conform to self-will that even more fear always results?"

"Yes."

"Do you realize that you are unhappy, especially when the external world doesn't follow your commands?"

"Yes."

"Do you realize that you can't seem to be of help to other people since, if you can't help yourself, how could you possibly help others?"

"Yes."

"Are you convinced, Floyd, that without some Higher Power you will continue to live a life based on self-will and that your self-will will keep creating the same reality you have been creating?"

"Mark, I have twenty-five years of drinking experience to confirm that point. I know that unless something different manifests through me, nothing will change."

"Good, Floyd. You're starting to remember what you already know, and you're starting to forget what you have learned. You see, Floyd, selfishness—self-centeredness—is what will kill you. Why? Because in that state-of-being, the universe which runs along the lines of God's Will shall not conform to your will. This creates the 'dis-ease' in you which we have spoken of; then your mind tells you to drink to treat the 'dis-ease' which your own self-will is creating. And your terrible dilemma is that you can't do anything about your self-will. Only this new Power can remove whatever self-will has separated you from experiencing your True Self. You see, Floyd, all of your troubles are of your own making. Now that might seem to be a disheartening statement at first glance, but in truth, that's the greatest statement of hope that you'll ever hear."

Pausing before he spoke—a rare experience for Floyd up to this point in his life—he considered Mark's statement and then still had to say, "Senseless. That's a totally senseless comment."

"Maybe. Let me explain, Floyd, and we'll see. You are a creator. You have created the 'reality' in which you are now living. That encompasses every area of your life, including drinking alcohol. It is a life created out of self-will, not out of the Will of the Universe. The end result is the life that you've been experiencing and living. Now, Floyd, do you like the life you've been experiencing and living, or do you want it to change?"

"I've already told you that I hate the life I've been living. I admitted that I've given it my best shot but I've still fallen short time and time again. But why would I think it's great if I create my own problems?"

"Because if anyone else were creating them—the way you've imagined—you're screwed. You really *would be* hopeless—which in fact you are not—because if others have been creating your problems, then they could continue to do so. But we've seen thousands get free of their problems by doing what's required to bring about a change of heart and a change of mind, and then their problems disappear. So the fact that *you* create your problems is great news. With that being the case, you have a chance."

Floyd remained quiet. Mark continued.

"So it's great that you hate the life you've been living and it's great that you are seeing you don't have the power to control yourself or others, Floyd, for it is from weakness that great strength comes. So here's your decision. From this moment on, are you willing to let God, as you now understand that Power, to be the Director in your life?"

"Yes, Mark, I am."

"The promise, Floyd, is that from this decision and the subsequent actions that you will take, God will remove your self-will and you will begin to live under the influence of that new Power. Along that line, Floyd, you can do anything. Keep on keeping on, my man. See ya."

"Yeah . . . see ya."

are you willing to let Dad be the director of your life?

CHAPTER 9—STEP FOUR

"I AM BORN"

"Since Paul is having trouble writing his fourth step, let's keep our comments restricted to that step today, please. Remember, in Step Four, we're invited to inventory our past behaviors and discover what part we played in creating our own problems. Floyd, since you had a great deal of trouble with your Fourth Step, would you like to start?"

"Sure. My name is Floyd, and I'm a *real alcoholic*."

"HI, FLOYD."

"Report is that I was wanted. Mom and Dad had supposedly worked as hard at getting pregnant as some work at avoiding that condition. At 9 pounds, 10-1/2 ounces, I would cause great pain from my first day on. I didn't know to what extent until I did my Fourth Step and the follow-up Fifth Step.

"The nurses taped a sign to my crib after I was born. It read, 'The Little Giant.' Such dichotomy and duality, such seeming contradiction, would characterize my entire life until I did the step work with Mark. I was the "little...giant," was "ecstatic and miserable," was "high and low," was "rich and broke," was "broke and rich." There was never any middle ground, never any balance in my life. There was only duality, a detachment from my True *SELF* and an attachment to the many false selves.

"My first name meant 'gray,' and I usually was. My chances for developing a good, positive mood were usually tempered by comments in my environment about the positive benefits of suicide.

My bad attitude and desire to self-destruct may have come from that influence, or I may have developed those tendencies on my own via my experiences. Some have even shown that there was an organic and chemical aspect to it as well. Regardless of cause or causes, I got 'em, but I certainly didn't want to tell anyone about them or about all of the horrible things I had done in my life. I procrastinated with working the steps because I had read ahead—I knew the plan for all these 'crimes' in Step Nine! Ha.

"How could I tell the folks here about the $80,000 I owed to three out-of-state firms? I had a great deal to hide, and if I contacted those people, I might die. If I did Four through Eight, I'd have to make those amends. Who am I? Rockefeller? Superman? I'm going to approach those people in one firm that I owed $60,000 plus the interest on the unpaid balance? How many millions does that come to? More than I could ever pay. No, there's no way I could mention that, but the anger and fear around it all made me miserable for years.

"And I got no help from the psychologist and his attempts to use hypnosis to straighten out my anger and hostility; in fact, I nearly punched him out when he started talking about drinking problems.

"I said, 'You know, Doc, I'm about done wasting my time with you. I'm starting to think *I* know more about counseling than you do.'

"That was when he really flipped my switch. He said, 'Floyd, in that case, if you're going to stop working with me, would you be willing to talk to a friend of mine who joined a fellowship because he's an alcoholic?' I said, 'Hey, Doc. Don't you think I've got enough crap going on in my own life than to spend my free time counseling some drunk friend of yours? You get paid to do this psycho-babble B.S.—*you* go talk to him."

"There were a lot of things about me that others saw that I simply could not see. As Cassius said to Brutus in Shakespeare's *Julius Caesar*, 'It is very much lamented that you have no mirrors...that you might see your shadow.' Eventually, I allowed Mark to be my mirror, and in seeing my shadows—my false personas—I was able to complete the journey of transformation and finally see my Real *SELF*."

"Mark's Analysis of
Floyd's Behavior — Step Four"

Seeing his shadow—seeing that which has been blocking the alcoholic from experiencing the light—is exactly what the Fourth Step is about. (The cover of this book illustrates the shift from the darkness to the light that I was trying to bring into Floyd's consciousness.) Having experienced the hopelessness of Step One through coming to realize that one has a multi-tiered disease of mind, body, emotions and spirit; having experienced the hope of Step Two through developing a willingness to believe in a Power greater than oneself; having formulated a new, personal concept of that Power; having made a choice that the new Power will be everything to him; and then having realized that he can experience and know that Power only within himself, then the alcoholic is able to make his Third Step decision.

That decision is based on the drunk's experience that any life based on self-will cannot and will not work; that the root of the drunk's problem is his self-will—that is, his selfishness—run riot; and he sees that, above everything, his selfishness must die or he will die. He has discovered that there is nothing that he can do about his own self-will, and he has accepted the fact that only God can remove self-will from the alcoholic; hence, the drunk makes the Third Step decision to turn his will and his life over to God as he understands that Power now. He then begins a three-part inventory which will encompass his efforts to face, and then rid himself of, the things which have blocked the alcoholic from experiencing and knowing a life lived in line with God's will. The protégé will begin to see the light, and the shadows will begin to fade.

Floyd will now write a resentment inventory, a fear inventory, and a sex inventory. These three inventories will show the alcoholic, and allow him to experience, how he has been playing God and how he has been living his life based on self-will. The end result of living a life on self-will is that the alcoholic becomes consumed with resentments because people and the world don't do what his self-will thinks they should. Resentment will follow, for self-will is only concerned with self, isn't it? Subsequently, the alcoholic becomes consumed with fear, the fear resulting from the fact that self-reliance has failed time and time again. When "self" does not get its way, it becomes both angry and afraid, so the very fabric of the alcoholic's life becomes an interwoven pattern of irritability and trepidation.

The sex inventory, in the final analysis, isn't really about sex. As in the case of the two other inventories, the sex inventory becomes another revealing analysis of a life run on self-will, of a life based in selfishness and self-centeredness.

The Fourth Step inventory is an action taken so that the alcoholic can experience who he is not, can experience Who He Is in order to move toward a consciousness of his True *SELF*, and can be rid of those things which have blocked him from flowing naturally with the Will of the Universe.

"MARK GUIDES HIS PROTÉGÉ THROUGH STEP FOUR"

"Well, Floyd, here we are again, you with your notebook in hand and with a sincere desire to get on with this Fourth Step. You do have a sincere desire to get on with this, don't you, Floyd? You look wary."

"To be honest, Mark, I've heard a lot of comments lately about this step, and most of them haven't made me feel too good."

"Floyd, you must always use discernment when hearing other people's opinions. The whole purpose of these three inventories is to face and then be rid of the things which have blocked you from knowing and experiencing the God of your new understanding. How can you not get excited about that? Remember what we've talked about: change your thought-life and you change the end result. Look forward to the writing of inventory because you will discover who you are not and you will experience who you have always been. The light of inventory will dispel the darkness, if you will; the light will dispel that 'shadow'."

"That idea I think I can work with. Explain the resentment inventory."

"Floyd, you're going to write a three-column resentment inventory. You're going to start in column one with a list of the people, institutions, and principles or rules that have angered you. Based on our conversations, coming up with a list of resentments should-n't be too hard for you, should it?"

"Funny, Mark. Real funny."

"Who comes to mind?"

"You mean like my ex-wife and people like that?"

"That's right, Floyd. Go ahead and write her name. Mark paused for a few moments to get his protégé involved in the writing. Then he continued.

"And once you've finished that list, we move on to column two where you write down why you're resentful at that person. In other words, you're going to write what you think they did that was wrong or what you think is wrong with them."

"I think I'll be able to write that second column pretty well," Floyd said confidently.

"I'm sure you will, Floyd. You'll feel right at home in that second column because you've lived there most of your life. You've always been a victim, always wanting to take no responsibility for your life and to blame others."

"Hey. You haven't always been around me," Floyd said as he raised his voice.

"You probably won't like my shattering your illusion of unique-ness, Floyd, but what I said is true for *all* alcoholics with this illness. Too many people want to assume no responsibility for their lives. It's always so easy to blame outside events and circumstances, isn't it?"

"Don't get personal, Mark. So what goes in the third column you mentioned?"

"Floyd, the third column is quite important since it holds the key to your entire future. Your drinking has been but a symptom. The third column will reveal the condition (the false state-of-being or ego-state) from which your resentments grew. It was always from an ego-state that you felt hurt, threatened, or interfered with in your efforts to get the things that each state-of-being believes it needs to exist, to *be*. Only from the assumed identity of an ego-state can hurt or threat or interference be imagined. So important is this column that we look at each state-of-being in seven specific areas.

"We begin with 'self-esteem' to identify how you feel and think about yourself, how you see yourself. The other areas include 'ambition,' seeing what each state-of-being wants; 'security,' identifying what each state-of-being thinks it needs in order to be OK, to exist; and 'personal relations,' asking what each ego-state wants in terms of relations with others. This part embodies your idea of how you think others in general are supposed to treat you, how you think they should act, what you think they should recognize about you. Then we go to 'sexual relations,' finding what your view is regarding how people of the opposite sex should be, how they should act, and how they should treat you. We then look at 'pride,' uncovering how you think others should view you; and then we look at 'money,' uncovering how your states-of-being perceive that you are being affected financially. The purpose of the third column, Floyd, is to turn the second column into a lie, to help you see how you were playing God.

"For example, I noticed earlier that in column one you wrote your ex-wife's name...'the ex.' Then in column two, you wrote that you resented her because, in divorcing you...how did you word it?"

"I wrote, 'She took everything that I had worked so hard to accumulate.'"

"Fine. Now, let's look at column three. Next to self-esteem, you listed an ego-state when you wrote, 'I am king of my castle; I should be in charge; I should decide who stays and who goes; I'm the bread winner.' So let's see what ambitions arose out of the state-of-being we'll call 'Floyd the Husband.' What does 'Floyd the Husband' want? And be honest."

"He wants to be left alone, Mark. He wants to be respected and honored."

"What does he need to be OK, Floyd, in terms of security?"

"He needs a wife. He needs his possessions. He needs to be in control."

Floyd suddenly paused, actually seeming to choke up for a

moment. Then he said, "You know, Mark, I'm starting to see some things now. Do you think that maybe I was as much at fault as she was?"

"Gee, Floyd, you think? Could that even be *possible*?! Ha."

Mark paused again, this time to give Floyd the full opportunity to enjoy the glare he was sending toward Mark. And in pausing, Mark modeled why those in relationship with an alcoholic cannot do this work with them. They cannot help in the fashion Mark helped Floyd. By pausing and not reacting, Mark modeled the necessary detachment. He understands the pent-up anger and hostility that alcoholics suffer, but he does not react to it himself. He understands the fact that those with untreated alcoholism will often be cruel to the very person who is trying to help and who is offering to save their lives. As one who has no attachment, Mark can serve his protégé effectively as he takes none of Floyd's reactions personally. Those involved with, in love with, concerned about, or suffering right along with the sick alcoholic seldom have the ability to detach and to ignore the meanness and cruelty and still continue to offer help unconditionally while taking none of the slams personally.

After Floyd lost the glare, Mark continued, "Floyd, using what you've learned so far, describe the state-of-being you were living in at the time your marriage was ending. Use some specific adjectives from this list," Mark requested, pointing to some lines in his book.

Looking at the passage in the book handed to him, Floyd said, "I guess in that state-of-being, I was...selfish."

"And?"

"And maybe...what is self-seeking?"

"*Seeking* things for your *self* all the time."

"OK. Then I was self-seeking."

"Anything else, Floyd?"

"Isn't that enough?"

"*Enough* is when we have *all* the truth, Floyd. Keep reading, keep reflecting."

"OK, there were times when I was dishonest."

"And?"

"And deep inside...."

"Yes, Floyd?"

"I've never admitted this to anyone, much less another man."

"Admit it."

"I was this one, too," Floyd said pointing.

"I can't see the book, Floyd. You need to say it."

Floyd turned the book toward Mark and pointed, but when Mark didn't respond, Floyd looked up to see that Mark had closed his eyes.

Damn, Floyd thought. Finally, he took a deep breath and said, "This one here. Fear. I've always been...afraid."

Mark opened his eyes and Floyd looked up to meet them. Then Floyd looked back down at the words on the page. After some time, he said just above a whisper, choking on a few of his words, "Yes. I was all of those. My gosh, Mark. I've been thinking all wrong. I've been living a lie."

"I know, Floyd. You've been experiencing who you are not. Now, you are just beginning to see Who You Are and what you can be. From this inventory, you can identity a lot of your fears, can't you? Name a few."

"I guess I had a fear of looking bad."

"What else?"

"Maybe a fear of being abandoned."

"Good, Floyd. Be honest with me, and be thorough. What else?"

"I've always had a fear of failure."

"I'll bet. Failure was never an acceptable option in your upbringing. What else?"

"I had a fear of not being loved. I feared making mistakes and being criticized," Floyd confessed quietly as tears began to stream down his face. Mark waited for the tear hanging from Floyd's lower jaw, watching it until it fell past his shirt and struck the leg of his jeans. He continued to pause long enough for the truth to manifest into Floyd's consciousness.

Finally, after Floyd used the back of his hand to wipe his face dry, Mark asked, "Do you see that these fears came because you tried to be self-reliant?"

Floyd had to think about that. "I guess from that...and some kind of dependence...and maybe some kind of sense of being inferior and not believing that I was good enough."

"But your self-reliance has failed you, hasn't it?"

"Yes," Floyd whispered, then grew completely quiet. Mark waited. "So you're saying that when I'm relying on self, then I'm into self-will, and if I don't get my way, I become afraid that I'll lose something that I have...or not get some result that I want?"

Mark tilted his head and raised his eyebrows as if to say, *Doesn't that seem obvious now?* Or maybe, *But I'm going to stay quiet and wait for you to see it.*

Ultimately, Floyd continued. "So you're saying my fear-based decisions are resulting in even more fear?"

Again, the silent tilt of his head was Mark's only reaction. He knew Floyd was going in the direction he wanted him to go. He gave him free rein.

Then Floyd said, again very quietly, "Man, what a terrible way to live."

Mark allowed the silence that followed that comment to continue for several moments to allow Floyd to truly *experience* the truth that he was seeing for the first time in his life.

Eventually, Mark said quietly, "Yes, it's a terrible way to live, Floyd. But I've got some good news for you. You don't have to experience that anymore—not if you do this step and the rest of them the way I suggest."

Pausing to consider the prospect of a different life, Floyd for the first time showed a sincere glimmer of hope. He actually seemed ready and willing to move on to get the benefits. He even asked, "OK—so what about this sex inventory, Mark?"

Mark smiled. He knew something really was going to shift in the perspective of this man seated before him. "Floyd, you're going to write out a brief paragraph on each relationship and then answer some questions about each, such as, 'Where was I dishonest, inconsiderate, selfish, suspicious, jealous, or guilty of doing things that aroused bitterness?' We also want to find the answer to the question, 'Where were you at fault, Floyd, and what should you have done instead?' The answers to those questions will give you a road map through your thought-life as well as into your behavior in the future. Any more questions, Floyd?"

"I don't guess so, Mark."

"I hope you're excited about facing the things which have been blocking you and then even more excited about being rid of a life based on self-will, a life doomed to 'dis-ease.' Are you ready to lift up that mirror so you can 'see the shadows' in order to finally see the light?"

"I'm ready."

"Well, Floyd, it's time to heat up the pen and paper. See you later."

"See you."

And after Mark closed the door behind him, it was inside the room that only Floyd heard the very quiet "thanks" that was spoken.

CHAPTER 10—STEP FIVE

"SOMETIMES, I THINK
I'D RATHER BE DRUNK"

"Hi, Wayne. You got a minute to talk?"

"Sure, Floyd. Hang on and let me go to the other phone—it'll be a little more private." A moment later, "OK, Floyd. What's going on?"

"I don't know what's going on. I know I feel like I'm about to go crazy. Mark talked with me about the insanity of this disease in Step Two. I thought I was past that. Things seemed to be going so well, but now I feel as if I've crashed."

"Something in particular happen?"

"No. I can't put my finger on any one thing. I just feel as if I were a pane of glass being held in the giant hands of the world. And I feel like those hands are using their thumbs to push me into some concave shape, bending me just to the edge of the breaking point. And it seems like, if one more person puts the slightest pressure on me, just one little push with the end of a finger against that pane, I'm going to shatter into a million tiny pieces. That's it. For the months I've been in the program, I've felt great after getting past that initial craving. But now, I've lost that feeling. I just feel like I'm going nuts."

"Floyd, I don't quite understand that admission. You've been in the program for months. You've shared on several steps that you've progressed through. Yet the recurring theme I've heard throughout your sharing has centered on your first wife. You've talked at length about how horrible she was to suggest that you might be 'going crazy' or 'going nuts.' Now you've just admitted the very same thing about yourself that you were attacking her for saying."

[Long pause] "Hello, Floyd. Are you still there?"

"Yeah, I'm here."

"Did you hear what I just said?"

"Yeah, I heard you. [Long pause again] Wayne…I've been dreaming about drinking. I wake up in the middle of the night screaming. I've broken out in cold sweats. I was thrilled during my early days in here because of the neat changes, the great things that had been going on with me. But that's not happening anymore. It's like the worst nightmare conceivable. I lie there after these dreams and think, 'If this is all there is to sobriety…I don't know, Wayne. Sometimes I think I'd rather be drunk."

"Floyd, if that's all there was to my sobriety, I think I'd rather be drunk, too. I understand that feeling. Now, you've sat in meetings for months and talked about writing inventory. Is there something you haven't told us?"

"What do you mean 'us'? It sounds like you're separating me from the group, like you guys are a part of something that I'm not a part of."

"Is that the way you feel?"

"Yeah, that's the way I feel, damn it!" [Anger mounts]

"Floyd, you've *talked* about working the steps. Tell me where you really are with your work through the steps."

[Long pause]

"Floyd?"

"Yeah, I'm thinking. OK, I started writing that Fourth Step and I stopped."

"We know, Floyd."

"There's that 'we' again."

"Yes, Floyd. It's going to be 'us' and 'you' until you really join us. So far you've been a guest, not a real member. But we have to let you follow the path you choose. We have to let you do everything you need to do to get low enough to reach out and take what we're offering."

"How'd you know, Wayne?"

"Know what?"

"That I haven't done my Fifth Step yet?"

"Floyd, we see something in the eyes when the payoff comes after the work. People don't look the same way they've looked before. There's just something different about them afterwards. Amigo, you don't have The Look."

Floyd remained quiet, knowing that to question Wayne's observation would be futile. Wayne continued.

"You see, Floyd, we know because once you do the Fourth and the Fifth and survive the shock of hearing the hard, cold truth, you won't be able to hide the happiness about what you've found— the excitement, the truth, the peace. When it really happens, we'll see it in your eyes. We'll see it on your face. You will have an experience that you can't hide, even if you try. You'll have something 10-fold greater than anything you can ever imagine. You won't be able to mask it; you'll no longer be able to hide the truth. Then, you'll be a member. Then, you'll no longer be a guest, just dropping by." After another pause, Wayne went on.

"Floyd, you mentioned a pane earlier. The only thing we see in your eyes so far *is* pain. So far, you've got pain because you've not done what it takes to find the real cause of your pain. And you'll also have pain if you go drink again. In fact, you only have two alternatives: either you do it the way we've suggested, or you go ahead and drink, chasing eventual death to the bitter end. Why don't you finish writing that Fourth Step? Call Mark right now and set up a time to do your Fifth Step. I'd like to talk more, but my family and I are sitting down for our mealtime and then we're going for our evening walk together in the park. Talk to you later, Bro."

"Yeah. Right, Wayne. You just go right ahead and have a great time."

"That we shall, amigo. That we shall." [Click]

"MARK'S ANALYSIS OF
FLOYD'S BEHAVIOR—STEP FIVE"

Having finished the writing of the resentment, fear, and sex inventories—an action taken to face and to be rid of that which has blocked the alcoholic from knowing and experiencing the God of his understanding—the alcoholic is now prepared to admit to himself, to God, and to another person the exact nature of his defects. Defects arise out of living a life driven by selfishness, manifested in self-seeking, self-pity and self-delusion. If one is driven, only an *illusion* of having choice can exist because to be driven—by definition—is to be moved or transported by someone or something else. [Ultimately, Floyd would see the truth of that observation by Mark. When one is driven, he would come to realize, one has no real choice; thus, free-will is suspended. When free-will is suspended, he would see, one becomes powerless. Floyd would eventually understand how one arrives in the fellowship having as his first step the need to admit to powerlessness. The progression with Floyd moved from being "driven by self will" to transitioning into "loss of choice and free-will" to experiencing a state of "complete powerlessness."]

The alcoholic must rid himself of the defects of selfishness, self-seeking, self-pity and self-delusion or he will begin again to experience his disease, becoming restless, irritable and discontented—all of which are inner conditions. He will become so uncomfortable—experiencing no inner peace—that the alcoholic mind will demand ease and comfort. The alcoholic feels like a piece of glass that is about to be "shattered into a million tiny pieces"; he feels like he is "going insane"; he has been "dreaming about drinking." It is his demand for ease and comfort which leads the alcoholic to think of his former solution—the drink—to help rid himself of this "dis-ease." Thus, we see the alcoholic saying: "Sometimes I think I'd rather be drunk." Deed (that is, action) results from thought, so the alcoholic will take action on that thought and drink unless a Power greater than himself can bring about a change of mind and heart. Hence, the alcoholic must pick up pen and paper and write these three inventories which will allow him to *experience* all of the ways that a life run on self-will creates resentments, fears, and selfish sexual conduct.

Self-will has produced states-of-being (ego-states, false identities, personas) which have their own imagined needs, their own belief systems, and their own desires which must be met if they are to exist, to *be*. Those states-of-being are so concerned with self-preservation and self-gratification that they drive the alcoholic into selfish and self-seeking behaviors. Such is the case when one does not know his Real *SELF* but imagines that his false selves and phony personas define who he is. *SELF*-transformation will manifest when the false identities are abandoned and the True *SELF* come into consciousness. These behaviors, then, place the alcoholic at odds with all people and with all events which do not satisfy the self-will of each particular state-of-being (such as "the state-of-being a spouse" or "the state-of-being an employee," for example.) If the alcoholic cannot face the fact that these phony states-of-being exist, and if he cannot take the action necessary to rid himself of those false identities, then he will drink, live miserably, or kill himself.

Thus, these states-of-being have the ability to kill. It is in the writing of the Fourth Step and the taking of the Fifth Step that one can begin to pull free from these states-of-being and begin to find out who he is *not*. Then one can begin to experience oneness, that is, the person can begin to find out Who He or She Really Is. In transforming from the dual or multiple personalities to knowing the one True *SELF*, the sense of being torn or split or "shattered into a million tiny pieces" just disappears. The person can begin to transform from living in the delusion of being driven by false identities and can begin to exercise the free-will that comes when one knows his True *SELF*. *This* is the process that Floyd and I now call "*SELF*-transformation." The alcoholic transforms from accepting many false selves or states-of-being or ego-states as his identity (or identities) and shifts into a state of consciousness in which he or she becomes aware of the Real *SELF*. Being awake, aware, and conscious is being awake to one's Real Identity, aware of Who One Really Is, conscious of one's True Identity and no longer living in the schizophrenic state of multiple but false identities.

"MARK GUIDES HIS PROTÉGÉ
THROUGH STEP FIVE"

"Floyd, let's you and me review why we're going to do this Fifth Step. We saw in Step One that you have an illness of body, mind, emotions and spirit and that no human power can treat a spiritual illness. You now know experientially that you are a *real alcoholic*. In Step Two, you became willing to believe in some Power greater than yourself. You also came up with a concept of that Power—that is, you got to *create* a new concept of God—and you have learned that the Power will be revealed to you when you remember your True *SELF* and abandon your false identities.

"Next, you became convinced that any life run on your self-will did not work in the past and will not work in the future; furthermore, you now know that selfishness must die and you decided to quit playing God. Next came the action in the writing of the inventories where you are going to face and be rid of the defects arising out of self-will which have blocked you. Do you understand, Floyd, that such is what you have been experiencing in the writing of your three inventories?"

"Mark, it was amazing. I could literally feel myself being pulled away from those states-of-being which my self-will had created. When I changed my thought-life through the writing of the inventories—from the notion that it was going to be a negative process to the notion that it was going to be beneficial—I began to create a new thought-life in which those states-of-being could be eliminated. It was incredible."

"Now, Floyd, do you see why we say that the Fifth Step is a life-and-death matter? It's not just that it's a step necessary in the process of assuring that you never drink again and thereby avoid death. It's much more than that. It's the *death* of who you are not—namely, a person or "persona" with a self-will running riot—and the life of Who You Really Are. Floyd, you now see how, in this program, we get to re-create our lives: we die the death of self-will and begin to create a new life along the lines of God's will. And along those lines, you can do anything. You can experience happiness; you can experience joy; you can experience freedom; you can experience a true sense of oneness. What a deal! And you only had to die an alcoholic death to experience the glory of being reborn into a new life. So let's look at your columns and see where self-will and false personas were running your life."

"RETURNING HOME"

Floyd's thoughts were racing:

I can't explain the way I feel right now. Part of me feels ecstatic while part of me feels destroyed. What am I experiencing? I'm dazed, perplexed, but I feel hopeful, maybe for the first time ever. This must be what some people are talking about when they describe their 'moment of epiphany.'

Yet I'm drained. There's the dichotomy, again. I feel relieved but beaten. It seems I've just tasted honey but have also swallowed some kind of bitter medicine. I feel victory is mine for the taking while sensing defeat. Something has happened. I feel as if I'm losing my mind. But wait. Mark said I needed to lose my mind. <u>My</u> mind.

I finished my Fifth Step just a short time ago with Mark. I can't believe what happened in that short time. I haven't cried in years, yet I cried—and in front of another man, for gosh sakes! How'd that happen? He told me to return home, to find a quiet place to spend an uninterrupted hour, and to do what it said in the literature. I've read Step Six. I've re-read the first Five. 'Wrongs.' 'Defects of character.' Now, 'shortcomings.' They all kept coming back. All the wrongs I've done. All the things I just knew I was right about...but now see how wrong my perception was.

What a unique concept Mark tossed out for me to consider: 'Maybe the world is not naturally hostile toward Floyd. Maybe the world isn't full of idiots. Maybe it was Floyd who was declaring war against millions. Maybe it was crazy to enter a war with those odds. Maybe Floyd is not the Chairman of the Board of the Universe, in charge of Space and Time. Maybe Floyd fought The War of Life and lost. Maybe it's crazy for Floyd to keep fighting a war that he has already lost. Maybe God can negotiate a peaceful settlement between the opposing forces: Floyd versus...his false selves. Floyd versus...everyone else. You see, Floyd—God's not going to change things for Floyd. This new Power you've found is going to change Floyd for things.'

There's a knock at the door.

I can't answer.

The phone rings.

I can't answer. What am I feeling? I can't answer.

It is certainly something I have never felt before. It's like I'm reborn. There's an element of wonder, of marvel to whatever this is I'm experiencing. I'm in a stupor, yet I feel more conscious, more aware than I have felt in my entire life. But I'm not totally sure what I'm aware of. I felt darkness; now I'm sensing some degree of light. This really is so scary, so unique, and so different from anything I can remember having felt before. It's like I've joined the journey of humanity and entered into the flow of sane living. Mark hugged me, told me to 'Do what I said,' and then he left. To give me an order or to tell me what to do would have been fighting words just a few days ago. Now I find myself listening to him willingly.

I suddenly feel as if someone has unbound me, as if the bindings I've seemingly worn all my life have been removed. I feel freer than I have ever felt before. What did Mark just do with me? I don't understand this. I don't understand this at all.

[Reading from the literature] *"Became entirely ready...."* [Long pause, then more thoughts.] *Whether I understand or not, I'm ready. I'm ready to start returning home. I want to go all the way back to the Real Floyd. Is that what Mark was talking about? If I can go all the way back to the Real Floyd, I can begin creating a new Reality? I can actually re-create my...SELF or at least experience that True SELF for a change?*

"MARK'S ANALYSIS OF
FLOYD'S BEHAVIOR—STEP SIX"

Having finished the Fifth Step, the alcoholic may have had certain spiritual beliefs, but now he begins to have a spiritual experience, an awakening to *SELF*. Floyd's description of that first hour after returning home evidences the dramatic nature of that first spiritual experience. You see, when an alcoholic takes the action in the first five steps, that alcoholic has begun a process of re-creating herself/himself. The way to re-create oneself is to follow the exact opposite path we followed when the falsehoods were created in the first place. The alcoholic, through his thought-life, words, and actions had created a reality in which he had doomed himself to die an alcoholic death. By the way—he doesn't have to take a drink to die an alcoholic death, since alcoholics have a far higher suicide rate than the general population. In order to reverse this process, the alcoholic must reverse the order of his creating; that is, he takes action first; that leads to a change in the words spoken, and that will lead to a change in thought-life.

Having finished the Fifth Step with another person, the alcoholic has begun to be pulled away from the states-of-being created by his self-will. It is those very states-of-being that have doomed the alcoholic to a life of "dis-ease" and drinking. By pulling away from those states, the alcoholic begins to experience oneness with the True *SELF*; his fears begin to fall away. Why? Because if there is no self-will, then there can be no fear. He begins to "feel freer than he ever felt before." He can be alone and at perfect peace and ease. And there is a big difference between being alone and being lonely. By pulling away from those states-of-being, the alcoholic then experiences a true knowing of God within for he has begun to experience the death of self-will and the birth of tapping into the Power within. The act of having God manifest through him has produced peace, as evidenced by his saying that he feels "as if the bindings I've seemingly worn all my life have been removed."

Returning home, the alcoholic reviews the work he has done so far. He asks himself the following: "Have I had a solid experience with the first five steps? Have I begun to experience God manifesting through me, meaning, do I *know* my True *SELF* now? Have the actions I have taken resulted in conscious contact with a Higher Power?"

Having answered these questions through the advantage of his new spiritual awareness, the alcoholic then looks at Step Six. In this step, he must ask himself if he is willing to let God remove from him the defects that his self-will created to sustain itself, to be. Then he must ask himself if he truly believes that God will remove these defects. You see, if the defects don't go, they will take the drunk back to a state of consciousness called the "spiritual malady," and in that state, he will drink.

Thus, the questions that the alcoholic must answer are important, aren't they? And so we meet with Floyd again.

"Mark Guides His Protégé through Step Six"

"So, Floyd, having experienced the first five steps by taking a course of action, we are squarely faced in the Sixth Step with making another choice about re-creating your life. I have asked you to write out a list of the behaviors and beliefs that have come from living a life based on self-will run riot...behaviors and beliefs that resulted in your having reaped what you have sown. Having looked at those behaviors and beliefs and the effects they had on you, on your loved ones, and on everyone around you, do you now want to change those behaviors and beliefs, Floyd?"

"No doubt about it, Mark."

"Do you want to re-create what you will reap from now on?"

"Yes I do, Mark."

"What do you now see that you were blind to in the past?"

"I see that the way I was living alienated everyone around me. I'm proof that a life driven by self-will can produce no peace, can produce nothing but discord. I see that only unhappiness and bitterness can follow. And I know that if those states-of-mind you described are in me, I *will* drink even when I don't want to. I finally understand what you meant when you said that booze was my solution and not my problem."

"Right, Floyd. Drinking treated the condition of spiritual illness. Booze was the only thing you knew of that would treat that state. My gosh, what a horrible way to live."

"The crazy part is that when people tried to help me, my thought-life was so twisted that I actually believed *they* were at fault. Now I understand what you mean when you say that all of my troubles are of my own making. I also understand what you mean when you say that is the greatest statement of hope I will ever hear, for I get to re-create that which I created which was all wrong. I see now that, if my problems were of someone else's making, I couldn't do anything about them, but since my problems are of my own making, I can stop doing the things that caused my troubles."

"Exactly. At least, you can *now*. Before, you were driven so you had no choice. You see, Floyd, by tapping into this newly-found Power, you can re-create a life and it can be a life filled with joy, peace, love, acceptance, and gratitude."

"I almost had to die of alcoholism to be reborn, to be given the gift of re-creating."

"So back to my question, Floyd. Are you willing for God to take away all of those behaviors and beliefs?"

"Mark, I'm completely ready."

"In that case, it sounds to me as if we can move on to Step Seven, Brother."

"Thanks, Mark. See you later."

"I'VE BEEN BLINDED BY THE LIGHT"

Mark answered his telephone.

"Hey Mark, what are you doing?"

"Talking to you."

"Have you got a minute?"

"Have you noticed that when you call, you ask for a minute but really want an hour?"

"I need to talk."

"Talk, Brother."

"Mark, I did what you said. I returned home. I know you said I may have had some spiritual beliefs before Step Five but that, after completing Five, I would have my first true spiritual experience. That was exactly the way it was as I returned home and did Six and Seven."

"Move ahead, Floyd. I don't have long right now."

"You told me a change of mind will come about. You also talked about *experiencing* the steps—really having an experience with each of them. I had that with Five. It was so powerful. I knew for the first time, I mean *really* knew, that I had been operating on self-will all my life and that there really is a better Floyd hidden under all those facades I used."

"Go on."

"You said my thought-life has to change, that my self-will cannot eliminate my self-will anymore than I can single-handedly overcome the power that alcohol held over me. I had no real understanding of what you were talking about until last night. In the state I entered, I not only saw my defects for the first time but I also really became entirely ready to have all those defects removed. I was, for the first time, able to look at that word 'humbly' that you told me to focus on in Step Seven and accept it. I did."

"Floyd, this all sounds great, so why have you called?"

"Because I humbled myself, dang it. Because I had some kind of experience in Four and Five and Six that I can't understand— but I had enough faith in this deal to go ahead anyway. Then I asked for my shortcomings to be removed."

"Sounds right so far."

"I felt cleansed afterwards. Years of guilt and disgrace and humiliation vanished. I felt I had really moved into a state of spiritual maturity."

Mark laughed, *really* laughed, not even attempting to answer.

"What's so dang funny?"

"That's something we'll need more time to talk about than I have right now. So, again, Floyd, why are you calling?"

"After all of that, I got up this morning, went downstairs to fix my coffee, and my wife had left a drawer open last night. I busted my leg on it, and I went into a rage. So why am I calling? I'm calling to say, 'What's the deal with this program? What's the deal with all your God talk?' I asked to have my shortcomings removed. I'm doing this deal the way I'm told. I'm working these steps, and yet this is what I get? We focused on my anger, my rage. I saw it. I asked for it to be removed and, BOOM! Here it is. I've still got it! I don't mind telling you, Mark, I've got some real doubts about this whole thing now. And I don't want to hear about 'demanding more from life than there is.' I want some answers, Mark. I haven't had a drink in years but I'm still going off on people. So have I changed or not? After asking this Power to remove these defects and then seeing them reappear, I'm really wondering again about the effectiveness of this whole program."

"Floyd, I told you that you were going to be enlightened by Steps Five, Six and Seven, not totally recovered by their end."

"The way I feel right now, I think I've been blinded by that light. We've thrown light on things I didn't want to see. Then I saw them. Then I wanted them to disappear. But they're still here."

"Well guess what, Floyd. I've got good news for you. There are five more steps. The program doesn't end with Seven, because if it did, we would all experience no more change or growth than you've experienced. Then we'd go drink and die; or we'd suffer untreated alcoholism that would eventually kill us without our ever having taken the first drink. I told you that 'your mind will take you into a strange mental blank spot where all your self-knowledge and willpower are unavailable to you.' I told you that 'If knowledge was your problem, you wouldn't be sitting down and talking to me.' If knowledge was your problem, you would never have met me. You *had* knowledge, probably more than was beneficial. Are you even listening to me?"

"I'm listening."

"Well, you don't seem to be remembering."

"Your attitude is really starting to bother me, Mark."

"Yeah, and what did I tell you about that? 'You're so sensitive, and that is a serious handicap that I hope you'll outgrow.' Do you remember that?"

Silence prevailed. Floyd made no response, so Mark continued.

"You see, Floyd, I told you that 'If there is not a complete change in your ideas (your thought-life), your emotions, and your attitudes, you will never recover and you will be doomed to die an alcoholic death.' You say you've changed. If the changes in you were adequate at this point to make you happy, joyous, and free, we wouldn't need any of the other steps. I want you to go sit down alone and work more on that list of behaviors and belief systems. We obviously have more work to do in those areas. Now I've got to go. I'm late for a jogging date at the park. Later. Goodbye."

"Yeah, right. You just go right ahead and have yourself a grand ole time."

"Indeed I shall, my friend. Indeed I shall." [Click]

"MARK'S ANALYSIS OF
FLOYD'S BEHAVIOR—STEP SEVEN"

In the Seventh Step, the alcoholic uses words to continue the process of re-creating his life with the guidance, protection, and help of the God of his understanding. He will ask for removal of all the things which he now admits are his liabilities and which stand in the way of his being happy, joyous, and free.

This is an act of humility, an act of love, through which the drunk begins to experience his oneness with his Real *SELF* and others and thereby begins to experience a sense of peace. The transformation from living in the delusion of the false selves—from playing false roles—begins. *SELF*-transformation also begins to manifest. The alcoholic begins to know Who He Really Is after seeing all the roles he played that were who he was *not*. The death of self-will through the process of Steps Four through Seven brings about a revolutionary change in the heart and mind. Through the process of working those steps, the alcoholic has been freed of his chains—of those things that have been binding him, if you will—for, ultimately, he was bound up by the bondage of self that he had created or that had been planted in his mind by way of faulty programming and wrong conditioning. He becomes aware of the fact that it is the false selves that bind us, and it is by rejecting those false roles as one's "true" identity that allows consciousness of the Real *SELF* to come into being. *That* is the "transformation," which is really only a shift from unconsciousness to consciousness, from believing the false selves were "real" to seeing that the false roles were indeed false. The drunk begins to see that he was unconscious not only when passed out from drinking but that he was unconscious even as he walked about in a supposed state of being awake.

The drunk begins to remember what he has always known, and he begins to leave behind what he is not. His change of heart and mind, combined with a change of actions and words, have all begun to lead to a re-creation in his life. This affords him freedom from the obsessive thought-life around drinking and from the detriment of having his life run on self-will. The alcoholic will experience a shift—a transformation, a re-creation—whereby he begins to experience his True *SELF*.

Once this step creates a feeling of oneness with *SELF* and with All, the drunk can start living a life in which he chooses to be conscious, to be awake, and to be aware. The morning after doing this part of the work, he is—with each beat of his heart—re-creating his life. He faces a choice: does he want to experience a life that runs along the lines of the Will of the Universe or does he want to begin to experience the rebirth of his self-will and all of the negative consequences that follow that? If the drunk does not walk in awareness, then his self-will will surely live again. Floyd evidenced the truth of that fact by continuing to "go off" on people. Having experienced the oneness with his Higher Power and with his Real *SELF*, the alcoholic can move on to Steps Eight and Nine through which he will begin to experience oneness with his fellow human beings and the Power of the Universe.

"Mark Guides His Protégé through Step Seven"

"Today, Floyd, you're going to take action in the Seventh Step in which you will humbly ask God as you now understand that Power to remove from you the defects—all those things that arose out of self-will. Why? Because those defects prevent you from being happy, joyous, and free. Because they separate you from knowing your True *SELF* and all else.

"But first, let's review the actions you have experienced up to this moment. In Step One, you found out what it means to be powerless over alcohol and to live an unmanageable life. You learned that you have a multi-faceted illness: first, of body since you have a physical allergy which manifests itself in a craving for more alcohol once you take the first drink. Secondly, you have an illness of the mind since you have a mind that lies to you again and again *when you are sober* and tells you that it is not only possible to have one drink but also that you will be able to control the amount that you drink—as if that is something you ever wanted to do. Thirdly, you experienced that you have an emotional sickness that leaves you emotionally intoxicated, even when you're not physically intoxicated. Finally, you have an illness of spirit since that spiritual illness creates 'dis-ease' within you, and then it is that 'dis-ease' which takes you back to a drink. You learned that the 'dis-ease' comes from living a life based in self-will, a dilemma that you can do nothing about on your own power. So in Step Two, you became willing to believe in a Power greater than yourself.

"You created a concept of a Higher Power that you could relate to. In Step Three, you made a decision to turn your will and your life over to that Power because of the truth you learned in Steps One and Two. In those steps you experienced the truth that any life run on self-will cannot work and because you knew that you needed help in re-creating your life.

"Your next action was to write the inventories which would show you what had been blocking you from experiencing and knowing Truth. You're taking a series of actions which have removed from you the things that have been keeping you from experiencing what has always been there—namely, your Real *SELF* and a sense of Oneness with All.

"Once you completed the three inventories and realized your defects (which were nothing more than the manifestations of your living a life based in self-will), we did a Fifth Step in which you admitted to God, to yourself, and to me the exact nature of your wrongs. In Step Six, we made a list of behaviors and belief systems— those things which fuel your behaviors—and you became willing for the God of your understanding to remove those defects. You realized that you could attain no permanent sobriety unless these defects were removed. Now, the literature says that 'many' of the people who worked the steps said certain words at this point. So now, I ask you, Floyd, are you willing? Are you now willing to be willing?"

"Yes, Mark, my life and my self-will have been a living hell. I'm experiencing some of the freedom from the bondage of self. I'm experiencing other states-of-mind that I've never experienced before. My whole life is being re-created."

"Then say the words, Floyd."

"I turn myself over to the care of my Higher Power. May all the defects that stand in the way be removed. Please let it be."

"WE'RE MAKING A LIST, WE'RE CHECKING IT TWICE"

"Yeah, I have a topic. My name is Floyd, and I'm a *real alcoholic*."

"HI, FLOYD."

"I need to talk about where I am in the work. I struggled with my movement through Six and Seven, as you know. I really fought the challenge of facing defects. The patience of my sponsor and my spiritual advisor has worked wonders for me. Weeks ago, I was furious with a friend who laughed when I said I had moved into a state of spiritual maturity."

An interruption of huge laughter came from around the table. Floyd paused, taken aback by the extent of the laughter. Then, he smiled and said, "OK—I deserve that. I was behaving somewhat better, so I thought I was owed something in return. I wanted to be rewarded for doing things that sane people do automatically. Overall, my thinking and my behaviors were not where they should have been—not by a long shot. So then they told me to make a list of persons I had harmed and prepare to make amends. I thought 'Yeah—and while I'm at it, I'll list all of the stars in the sky.' I owe $60,000 to a bunch that will file charges against me or will kill me and $20,000 to two other companies. And if I'm not killed, none of that will matter anyway since I can't pay off $80 right now, much less $80,000.' But I have to change my thought-life if I'm to reach a state that will take me out of this restless, irritable, and discontented condition that I'm in. I know I have to do the steps the way Mark is showing me if I'm going to move to a higher level. I know what the next level is, and I'm going to get there. I'm facing a real challenge as I prepare to humble myself in amends-making. I have no idea where I'm headed in facing $80,000 in debt, but Mark showed me that if I begin, the Power will bring it to a proper end. So based on that faith alone, I'm going to enter into Eight and Nine.

"For the first time in my life, I don't feel totally isolated and alone. I know I'm having some kind of spiritual experience, but I still haven't had that complete awakening yet, that complete change. So no matter how distasteful I think the next step is going to be, I'm going to do it. I'm really starting to believe that I just might be able to do this thing. Thanks for letting me share."

"MARK'S ANALYSIS OF FLOYD'S BEHAVIOR—STEP EIGHT"

In the Eighth Step, alcoholics are asked to make a list of all the people they have harmed. The alcoholic must also become willing to make amends to *all* of those people. By this time he has begun to undergo a dramatic experience that is resulting in a change of heart and mind. Remember our definition of 'sanity'? Having completed the actions in the first seven steps, the alcoholic has commenced to experience conscious contact with "Right Thinking," with sanity. He has begun to feel at one with All. Feeling "at one," he no longer feels like he's "a million pieces."

This list becomes vitally important as it will be a necessary element in the upcoming action that is necessary for the alcoholic to experience oneness with the Power, with his fellow human beings and with all things in this world and the universe. You see, the alcoholic has an ego that has three motives: it wants first to separate the alcoholic from knowing the truth and to allow the alcoholic ego to think it is God. Next, that ego wants to separate him from knowing his True *SELF*. Finally, that ego wants to separate him from all others. That is its sole function—to convince the alcoholic of his uniqueness. If it can accomplish its mission, the alcoholic ego will create so much 'dis-ease' within the alcoholic that he will be driven to drink again, regardless of circumstances or consequences.

It is at this time that the protégé sits down with pen and paper and begins to expand his list of the people and the institutions that he has wronged in his lifetime. He also expands his study of the principles—the rules and laws—that he has resented and has violated. He will attempt to recall any harm that he has ever put out into the universe so that he can try to right that harm and thereby begin the process of experiencing oneness with all things.

Thus, he's making a list and he's checking it twice (or three times, or a dozen times, or more), to be certain that it contains all harms done, for the amends-making must be thorough and complete if the drunk's recovery is to be thorough and complete.

"Mark Guides His Protégé through Step Eight"

"Floyd, good to see you again. Time to get out your pencil and paper now as we have another list to fill out."

"You know, Mark, a guy could get tired of all these lists. I've made a list of resentments, a list of fears, a list of selfish relationships, a list of behaviors, a list of belief systems, and now another list of people I'm going to make amends to. This is hard."

Quietly, almost whispering, Mark asked softly, "Floyd, do you remember what your life was like when you were drinking?"

"Sure."

"*That's* hard!" Mark screamed. "*This* is a damn cakewalk compared to that!"

After many moments of consideration in the quiet, Floyd finally concurred. "You're right, Mark. Sorry about the whining."

"Floyd, do you remember the change in thought-life that we've been talking about? This is another list to be *excited about*, not to be dreaded. By the way, Floyd. It isn't going to just be a list of people."

"What do you mean?"

"Floyd, we have a relationship with *all* things, so we will put *all* things harmed on the list. Let's start with B.J. Write down his name."

"B.J., my dog?"

"Yes, B.J., your dog."

Floyd shook his head, convinced that he wasn't the only guy in the room still able to come up with crazy ideas. But he wrote anyway. After he looked up from the paper, Mark continued. "From him, we'll also start our list of people you owe amends to. You see, you taught him to attack innocent people, so the first thing you need to do is make amends to him by making him kinder and allowing him to be happier instead of at war. Related to him, add to the list the names of your ex, your ex-mother-in-law, the vet and his assistants, and the gas meter reader you punched out because of B.J."

After reflecting on all of the past chaos generated just around his dog alone, Floyd finally said, "Damn, I was a jerk, wasn't I?"

"Right you are, Brother, but do The Work and you'll never have to be a jerk like that again. Start by treating all animals better. Start taking better care of pets. Teach your pets to love instead of to hate. Then continue with the list. This list, Floyd, will be a list of all harms that you have put out into the universe, all harms you have created through your self-willed actions. It will be a list of people, places, institutions, animals, anything you ever had a relationship with, Floyd, when you created harm."

"This could be tiring."

Exhaling quietly and pausing to guard his tongue, Mark said, "You tire *me*, Floyd. I thought the whining was over. Listen—just as it took you many years to produce the fields of wreckage that you created, so it may take you years to right it. But it *can* be done with your newly-found Power. You see, Floyd, we've been separated and fragmented our whole lives. These steps are about oneness: oneness with the Power; oneness with our True *SELF*; oneness with all others; oneness with all things. People who do not make amends, Floyd, will not experience their oneness; hence, they will always feel apart *from* instead of a part *of*. They will always feel separated and fragmented.

"When you realize in your heart, Floyd, that you and I are one, then you will realize that there is no action that you will ever want to take that can harm me because, with our being one, you also will experience that harm as well. You will realize that any harm you put out into the universe will eventually harm you. Now if anyone puts out harm into the universe, knowing that the harm he is putting out is also going to harm himself, then that person must be spiritually sick—insane—if he is willing to hurt himself. It would be like kicking yourself. I saw in your past a willingness to self-harm, evidenced in those episodes you described from your drinking days. In harming your first mother-in-law, you ended up experiencing the harm yourself. Remember when I told you that you will always reap what you sow?"

"Whoa. Mark, you're getting smarter every time I talk to you."

"Maybe. Or maybe you're getting smarter, or at least saner. I've told you that we are to love our neighbors as we love ourselves. Are you seeing the truth in that? Are you seeing the value in that now?"

"I really am, Mark."

"Good. I've gotta go. You know what you need to do. See you."

"Hey, Mark...thanks."

"Keep on keeping on, Brother."

"SWEEPING UP MY SIDE OF THE STREET"

Mark answers his telephone.

"Hey, Mark. Got a minute?"

"Not really—what's going on, Floyd?"

"Houston, we have a problem!"

"No, *we* don't have a problem. I'm doing quite well, thank you."

"Mark, I've got to come over. I'm furious."

"What now?"

"I started my amends, and one gal has really made me livid."

"Let's see, Floyd. What is today?"

"Tuesday."

"Tell you what—I'll meet you Friday and we can go over that."

"Friday? *Friday*! Heck, by Friday, I'll have forgotten all the details!"

"That's right."

"Mark, this is serious. Listen. I go to the secretary in our office and tell her that I have treated her like dirt all these years. I admit that I was egotistical, acting like I was better and raising my voice at her and generally making her life miserable. I told her that I wanted to apologize and say that I'm sorry and hope never to let it happen again."

"Sounds OK to me. So?"

"So she says nothing. Her mouth is just hanging open in shock. Her eyes almost roll back in her head. Then she says, 'Thank you. I can't believe what I'm hearing, but thank you.' Then a little smile came across her face, but she was still stunned."

"What's the matter with any of that?"

"Nothing. Then I go to the second secretary. Same thing."

"Two for two. You're on a roll. The problem is...?"

"Then I go to the third secretary and say the same thing, and get this. She says, 'Get out of my office, and don't ever come back, and don't ever speak to me again.' Can you believe that?"

"Heck yeah I can believe it. At least half the time, I want to tell you the same thing."

Silence prevails. Then Floyd said, "I'm serious, Mark. This amends-making stuff is a bunch of crap. Am I supposed to have to put up with this kind of garbage? What am I? A doormat now? Is that the plan in here? Let's make a doormat out of Floyd and then walk all over him?"

Floyd, you need to read the book, son. We stand on our feet. We don't crawl before anyone."

"So what do I do with this last gal?"

"What do you want to do with her?"

"I wanna kill her."

"I haven't come across that amends-making option in any of the literature I've read."

"So what am I going to do?"

"Tell me again what she said."

"She said, 'Get out of my office, and don't ever come back, and don't ever speak to me again'!"

"OK, then what you're going to do is stay out of her office, and don't ever go back, and don't ever speak to her again. Anything else I can do for you?"

"What?! She yelled that comment loud enough for everyone else in the office to hear? She made me look foolish."

"Ha. Did you ever yell at her loud enough for everyone else in the office to hear? Did you ever make her look foolish?" Silence dominates again.

"Hello, Floyd. Are you there?"

"Yeah, I'm here."

"Floyd, do you realize that nothing worthwhile can be accomplished until we do this step thoroughly and completely? We've talked about that in detail, haven't we? What happened to that 'I've had some spiritual experiences but I'm willing to do these steps so I can have a spiritual awakening'? What happened to that 'I want to get into the realm of the spirit'? You're on a journey into that realm, yet you're going to let one refusal of one amends stop your work in its tracks? You need to think about this. Have you swept up your side of that street? If you have, leave her side of the street alone.

"Floyd, you're not in charge of both sides of the street anymore. You're not in charge of her. And it doesn't sound like you're in charge of yourself right now, either. Somehow, I don't see a judge saying to Floyd, 'Oh, gee, Floyd. She refused to accept an apology after you humbled yourself by offering it? *Justifiable homicide! Boom! Case dismissed!*' I may be wrong, but I don't think that's what the judge will say. Of course, you've been before more judges than I have, so maybe you know more about it than I do. How do you expect to face an $80,000 amends if you can't face a woman telling you she doesn't want to talk to you? You told me when we went over your completed list that she hasn't talked to you in five years, for gosh sakes. What's going to be different now? Only you, if you let this go. Now I've got go. I'm doing the First Step with a newcomer tonight. See you later."

"Yeah, later."

"MARK'S ANALYSIS OF FLOYD'S BEHAVIOR—STEP NINE"

In this step, the alcoholic begins to make amends (that is, "to set things right") for the harms that he has put out into the universe. Whenever possible, he will make these amends face-to-face. After all, that's usually how the damage was created. In the previous step, the drunk made a list of all harms that he has put out into the universe. The list will include harms to mom, dad, brothers, sisters, wives, children, friends, employers, employees, people he owes money, animals, plants, nature, and the environment in general. In short, he will make a list of everything that he can possibly recall where his actions resulted in harm.

He is now going to take a series of actions to re-create in a positive way all of that which he created while being unconscious, and then he will begin living with the positive effects of his new creations. That is, he will now begin to re-create consciously by making direct amends. He will carefully review all amends with his advisor in order to insure that, in the process, he does not create more harm. Then he will begin the process of re-creating his reality.

On the top of his list, he has a name. He also has a thought, which is 'I am going to call this person and set right this wrong.' Next, he makes the call, so words are spoken. Then he sets an appointment and takes the action of meeting with the person and making the amends; thus, through thought, word, and deed, he is consciously taking actions to experience his oneness with his True *SELF* and with All. He is careful not to attach to the outcome of the amends. Because Floyd forgot this important point, he experienced a self-imposed crisis when one of his amends was not accepted. He must understand that his only role in the process is to show up and offer the amends. When the amends process is complete, he will have begun to experience oneness and to re-create consciously the effects of his unconscious creations in the past.

"Mark Guides His Protégé through Step Nine"

"Well, Floyd, you are more than halfway through your long list of amends, so it's time we talked about some of your expectations. You made a list of people, institutions, and principles through which you put out harms into the universe. You have been taking the necessary action to make direct amends and to re-create the relationships that were broken by your actions. What kind of experiences have you had?"

"Well, after getting past the silly hurdle with that third secretary who didn't react the way I wanted, and after realizing what you said is right—that my part is just to show up and make the amends—the whole process has been incredible."

"What's the most impressive result so far?"

"Well, I'll tell you later about the $80,000.00. I guess it'd have to be the results of that amends that was the most unexpected. I was dreading getting killed over that one, not to mention wondering how I could ever come up with that sum. And I told you about the willingness of two credit card companies to work out an unbelievably lenient payoff plan until I'm able to pay more."

"How about the amends with your family members? How are those going?"

"My amends with them and my friends have been wonderful. Dad and I are not just on speaking terms—we're really getting along. Some old relationships have begun again on a different standing and some others just went away. I'm OK with that, too, because you finally got it into my head that I have to detach from trying to control the outcome."

"What about the ex-wife? She certainly came up often in our work through those early steps when your resentments were being verbalized."

"I had to use the phone for that one. I called her long-distance and she not only accepted the amends but she said that she'd been wanting to speak to me. She said that she wanted to ask me to forgive the role she played in our troubles. Seventeen years I slammed her and begrudged her, but all those years of negative feelings and thoughts and words disappeared with a single phone call. Gone! It's amazing. I'll tell you, Mark, my sense of being at peace and at ease with all people has been taken to a level that I could never have even imagined. You were so right in what you said would result from these efforts."

"That's because you have begun, at a deep level, to experience your oneness with all things."

"You bet. And I've begun to understand that not once did I or anyone else ever wake up and decide that they were going to go out that day and try to harm someone intentionally. I see how we can be driven, and I see now that we just didn't understand that any time we harm anyone or anything, we're harming ourselves since we are at one with all things. I see that if we had known that, and experienced that, then we would never have taken the action to create the harm in the first place. By cleaning up my side of the street, I'm undoing the effects that I lived with when I was being driven by self-will. The peace within my heart, the stillness within my mind, and the love being manifested in my behavior toward others is a wonderful thing to experience and to behold. It may take me years to get through all these amends, but I'm willing because you've shown me how everything is connected to everything else."

"Has 'love thy neighbor as thyself' taken on a new level of meaning for you?"

"Not only that, but you're convinced me that I really do 'reap what I sow.' I'm now sowing good stuff. What a deal."

"What a deal, Floyd. What a deal, indeed."

"PASSING THROUGH THE WILDERNESS"

"OK—so the topic is 'The Promises.' Who wants to share?" The chairperson paused, then said, "How about you, Floyd?"

"OK. Hi. My name is Floyd, and I'm a *real alcoholic*."

"HI FLOYD."

"What I'd like to tell Bill is that I can relate to your struggling. I fought it like I fought the whole world before I really started working these steps. But I can promise you this about 'The Promises': they really *will* start coming true before you're even halfway through making your amends, and then the Tenth Step Promises kick in, too. [Deep, booming laughter comes from someone to the side.]

Floyd responds, "Yeah, Mark, go ahead and laugh. Mark knows how I fought the very step that was going to open the door to those two sets of promises for me. But for me, the destruction of self that comes from amends-making and regular personal inventory is so outweighed by the joys of receiving those promises that I regret ever having delayed. I was facing $80,000 in debt and I was broke. How long ago was that, Mark?"

"About a year, now."

"So about a year ago, I tell Mark I can't contact the dangerous people I owed $60,000 of that $80,000 total debt. I even told him that the owners deserved it because 'they were crooks themselves.' What a justification, huh? And he asked me, 'Did the stockholders deserve it'? 'Did the investors who are getting less in dividends and interest deserve it'? And the answer was 'No—they didn't deserve it.' So we set about to make the best deal possible, just as the literature says. I began by contacting a lawyer in that city. He agreed to try to work out a settlement plan, and I only had to come up with his $300 retainer to get started. And you know what he worked out for me? The original guys I had dealt with were gone, many of them jailed. The new guys with that firm had written the debt off and gotten tax credits, and—bottom line—they were done with the debt and were not interested in pursuing it. I have no one hunting me now and a $60,000 debt was forgiven! Of course my celebration was short-lived. Mark suggested that 'I took that out of the universe and I needed to put it back,' so the monthly money I'd have used to pay on that debt I am now giving to charities.

"If I hadn't taken the Ninth Step, and continued to live in the Tenth, I would still be looking over my shoulder, living in fear and drinking to drown it. It all disappeared in a couple of months, once I started. Mark is my witness. Mark?"

"It's true."

"Then the lawyer started on the $20,000 I owed to two banks for my credit card debt, telling their representatives of the changes I was trying to make in my life. The final deal? They froze all interest charges. Each agreed to accept $25 per month until I could pay more. And the lawyer? I had accrued several thousand dollars in bills for services he rendered to me. But he said that the $300 I sent him up front would do. He told me, 'I want to thank you for letting me be a part of what you're doing—I've never seen anything like this in my life.' Now get this. My business expanded and I sent him the balance last month to pay off both card companies. And I have credit cards from both those banks in my wallet right now.

"Is it going to stay this great? I have no idea what's in store for me. Are you going to get as good a deal? I have no idea what's in store for you. But I will tell you this: it is greater than anything you can imagine, if you turn it over and work these steps precisely as told.

"I'll end with this. I recently read the definition of 'wilderness.' It said, 'an uncultivated region of waste.' Then I read the definition of the same word in the original Hebrew, which meant, 'a region to be passed through.' See, I spent my entire life before recovery in the wilderness. I thought that was all there was, that this world was one big wasteland and that I had to stay in that region of waste. But I know the original meaning of 'wilderness' now. It's a place that I should have passed through, and I should have passed through it long before I did. None of us have to take that long.

"Today, I try to stay out of that wilderness by checking myself frequently. Of course I still make mistakes, plenty of them, but I know now that I'm capable of making *any* amends, so it's easy for me to make them quickly. When my mistakes put me back into the wilderness, my quick inventory and quick apology make sure that I'm only passing through the wilderness—not living in it again. Today, anger is no longer a stimulant; today, rage has lost its excitement; when I pull into my drive nowadays, my daughter is at the door to greet me, happy to see me. If we want 'The Promises,' we work the steps. It's become pretty simple for me. It's as if I were bound up all my life, but now it's like Mark's guidance and my efforts have removed the bindings that were keeping me from being free.

"I've also seen that two entirely different types of inventory exist in the steps. The first inventory I did with Mark was a 'moral inventory.' 'Moral' deals with 'right' and 'wrong'—not to label me as 'wrong' or 'bad' but to show me where my harmful behavior was not productive, not healthy or not constructive. I came to see that this Tenth Step was about something totally different. For me, I saw that for a considerable time after working the steps in the proper fashion with Mark, I still needed to take a 'personal inventory' regularly.

"Once the transformation occurred after I saw all the false selves, all of the false *personas* that were driving me, I came to know my True *SELF*, the Real *SELF*. This Tenth Step invites me to continue to take a personal inventory—an inventory of the *personas* that show back up. I know that I have entered one of those 'states-of-being'—one of those 'false *personas*'—when I am restless, irritable, discontent, bored, or emotionally intoxicated. Why? Because in my experience only an ego-state can experience the emotions that the literature told me to 'cast aside.' The Real *SELF* can experience the *feelings* that the literature promises will come back to me, but only my false *personas* inspire emotional reactions, and reactions to those reactions, and reactions to those reactions, *ad infinitum*. Today, I understand why analysts used the Latin word 'ego' (meaning 'I') to identify the 'false I,' the false self or selves. Thanks for letting me share."

"Mark's Analysis of Floyd's Behavior—Step Ten"

Having begun the action of making direct amends, the alcoholic has begun to re-create his life through a specific course of actions, taken in regard to all people and things which suffered ill effects from having contact with our alcoholic. That action requires that the alcoholic sit across from all people harmed when possible and that he set right the wrong he created when he was unconscious, not awake, or unaware. Such was the time when he was experiencing life through the effects of his creation but when he was not aware of his creation. That excluded him from consciously taking part in a positive creation process. Making amends provides the opportunity for true healing of all parties involved, even though it might not seem that way at the time to the alcoholic. Floyd had to learn that lesson when his third amends didn't go the way he planned.

Having commenced the course of action, the alcoholic also begins immediately the action of Step Ten in which he begins to take a personal inventory on a daily basis. Through this exercise, he will become aware of what he is creating via thought, word, and deed and will be ready to set right, promptly, any wrongs committed. He has, by this point, entered into the World of the Spirit; that is, he is now in conscious contact with his own conception of God, with others, and with his True *SELF*. *SELF*-transformation takes a huge leap forward. His entire purpose now is to grow in understanding and effectiveness in the World of the Spirit, meaning he is to be acutely conscious of what he is now creating. He begins to watch, mindfully, for evidence of selfishness, dishonesty, resentment, and fear. When he sees any of those effects of his false states-of-being begin to arise, he immediately takes the action for those to be removed.

If another person is involved in the alcoholic's having entered into those states, he talks to them if possible and he immediately sets right the wrong he has created, whether it came into existence through thought, word, or deed. He has ceased fighting anybody or anything; he is conscious; he is experiencing a sense of Oneness; he is aware of the fact that he is being guided throughout the course of the day by a new force. He has become awake to the fact that each part of his existence—the Spirit, the Emotions, the Mind, and the Body—have impacts that are all unequivocally real. He has begun to take a healthier course of action with his body that has also led to changes in both his thought-life as well as in the words he now uses. He has entered the World of the Spirit. In that world, Floyd is experiencing oneness with his Higher Power, oneness with his True *SELF*, and oneness with all things and all people. Now, for the first time, full integration of Body, Mind, and Spirit materializes. To maintain that state of existence, the alcoholic will continue an exciting and constructively creative process, actively looking for and identifying any false personas that might arise until he fixates in the full and final understanding of Who He Really Is.

"MARK GUIDES HIS PROTÉGÉ THROUGH STEP TEN"

"So, Floyd, we meet again, and I've noticed that you're the one who now sets the meeting and seems to be excited about the things that you're re-creating in your life."

"Mark, to watch this new consciousness manifest through me has been the most exciting experience of my life. The occurrences in the amends process have produced exactly what you said they would: a sense of oneness with all things, a loss of desire to influence people's lives unless they invite me to do so, and a great sense of peace. I also have a deep conviction that everything really is going to be all right. And I'm excited about what I know of the Tenth Step so far."

"Floyd, the fact that you want direction is further evidence of how far you've come since we first met."

"You just can't stop reminding me, can you?!"

"We've talked about having lived most of our lives with the negative effects of what we've been creating. We've been asleep and unaware. As you have taken the action through the first nine steps, you have begun to re-create your life in a positive fashion. Remember how we talked about the fact that we're constantly creating through thought, word, and deed? Remember how we've talked about the three elements that make up your one true being: the Body, the Mind, and the Spirit?"

"You bet."

"Well now in Step Ten, you're entering into the World of the Spirit. You are becoming conscious—conscious of God, of Power, of your Real *SELF*, of All. Along that line, you're going to start paying attention to every thought you have, to every word that you utter, and to every action that you take. Along the line of the Will of the Universe, you can do anything. The goal now is to be awake and to watch for manifestations of self-will because manifestations of the Will of the Universe and manifestations of your self-will are not compatible. They cannot co-exist. Only one can manifest in any person at any given time.

"And those manifestations of your self-will should now be easy to spot: they assume the form of fear, selfishness, dishonesty, or resentment. Those are the real manifestations of self, the actual results of assuming a false identity. Once you become aware of them, you turn toward good. You seek out someone else to help, for helping another human being pulls you out of self and into a state of existence called 'Love.' In that state, you cease fighting anything or anyone; you embrace all things and all people; you honor all things and all people. You even honor how you feel. In fact, you welcome how you feel—you treat that condition with honor; you pay attention to it; you let go of those things that bind you; you experience true freedom and love. You become aware of when you are being judgmental and you shift out of that state as soon as you become aware of the fact that you're experiencing it.

You will know that you do not know the intent of the soul in front of you, and you will look for the good within all people and all things because you are in oneness with them all."

"You're saying that there's a unity beyond all of the seeming multiplicity of things and people in our universe."

"Exactly, and we experience that unity when conscious of our oneness with All. Now, Floyd, to the next issue: have you experienced being placed in a neutral zone when it comes to alcohol?"

"I have, Mark, but I haven't been able to understand that."

"Well, Floyd, here's what has happened. Remember that your problem was that you were suffering 'dis-ease.' You were in varied states-of-being that resulted in your living a life based on self-will. The actions that you have taken through the first nine steps have removed the 'dis-ease' that existed within you."

"But you said I'd never be cured."

"You will never be cured of alcoholism, Floyd, because the body allergy is physical and cannot be changed. But you will exist in a state of consciousness—of Body, Mind and Spirit—in which you are completely recovered from alcoholism. And you will maintain that state by staying in fit spiritual condition and then paying attention to the other levels of sobriety that we'll discuss in the future."

"What's 'fit spiritual condition'?"

"Floyd, you look like you might have been an athlete at one time."

"What do you mean 'might have been'?!"

"Just answer the question, Floyd, and keep it short."

"Yeah, I played football and ran track."

"Floyd, if you had only worked out one time a week, or if you had only worked out for five minutes per day, what kind of physical shape would you have been in?"

"I would have been in terrible shape."

"Do you think you would have been prepared to face everything that you would come across in your sports activities?"

"I wouldn't have been in shape to face anything."

"Well, use the same analogy with your spiritual condition.

There's a course of action that you'll take in order to discipline yourself. The end result is that you will be in fit spiritual condition and you'll be ready to face anything that you come across. Along that line, your thought-life will constantly be inspiring you to ask, 'What would Love have me do?' You will have awakened a part of your being that you have previously been asleep to."

"You've talked earlier about 'spiritual experiences'—now you're talking about 'spiritual awakening'."

"See the difference now, Floyd?"

"Man, do I ever."

"Do you remember during our early days of working together, I asked you what it meant to 'be sober'?"

"Sure."

"And what did you answer?"

"I think I said it meant 'not drunk'."

"What do you think it means now?"

"I think it means 'aware, awake, conscious, showing good judgment'."

"Good work, Floyd. See, by going through this course of action, you have now awakened your spirit, and your spirit will always know what to do because its entire nature is to be a spirit of love. Alongside any event or question, then, you are to ask yourself, 'What would Love do?' The answer will always come to you. In the meantime, remember this: the experience of the experience is more important that the explanation of the experience. Just enjoy, Floyd. Just enjoy. See you next week."

"Yeah, see you next week, Mark. Bye."

CHAPTER 16—STEP ELEVEN

"OUR DAILY BREAD"

"Hello, Floyd. This is Dave."

"Hello, Dave."

"What are you doing, Floyd?"

"Talking to you."

"Yeah, I need to talk. I've been sharing some things at meetings, things we've talked about. You know, Floyd, as well-meaning as a lot of people are, they're sharing things that aren't in the literature. And when I speak to the contrary, they want to kill me. I mean, they really ate my lunch today."

"Remember, Dave, we need the fellowship; the fellowship doesn't need us. I forgot that for a time myself."

"I know that, Floyd. But it's so hard to sit there with a newcomer hearing one guy say 'take it slow and easy' and hearing the next guy tell him 'to seek it with the desperation of a drowning man.' The poor guy walked out in a daze."

"Did you grab him?"

"Yeah, we're meeting tomorrow to start going through the steps."

"Then you've done exactly what you were supposed to do, Dave. Remember, we don't just have *real alcoholics* in here. The moderate or hard drinkers can quit on a non-spiritual basis and without all the step work required for *real alcoholics*. Our founders cautioned us about that."

"Yeah, I don't listen to the hard drinkers, but they're killing some of these new guys."

"Dave, I know you're worried about the new guys, but it sounds like you might be more worried about the group turning on you when you shared a truth that contradicted some of the myths you've heard around the tables all these years. Sure, the middle-of-the-road solutions are killing people, but I sense you're not as worried about the new guy as you are what the group thinks of Dave. The new guy you're going to set straight tomorrow. Sounds like its Dave who needs to get set straight tonight. I seem to be hearing words coming from some state-of-being, like 'Dave the Fellowship Giant" or "Dave the Guy in Charge of Straightening Out Everyone and Everything."

"I hadn't thought of it that way."

"It seems that some ego-state has manifested and you're under the influence of one or more personas or false roles that we've discussed. And remember what I showed you, Dave. Those false roles were the prerequisite for the misery that set us up to seek booze and other things to help us escape the false lives and the lies we led when self-will was running riot. Today, when free of those identities, we can speak the truth and then let the chips fall where they may because only ego-states are attached to outcome and trying to control results."

Dave remained quiet, obviously considering the reminders, so Floyd allowed time for that deliberation. Then he continued, "You see, Dave, a friend in the program once explained to me how we get freedom from being bothered by experiences like the one you just had: it's none of my business what you or anyone else thinks about me. It's *my* business what I think about everyone else. I have to love or at least accept. Tolerance is a key that opens the door to peace, and I have to practice that even if I don't like your behavior. Now, Dave, if I put out love and then get love in return…fine. But if I don't, there are no negatives involved. Since it's none of my business what others think about me, I can't be adversely affected by their appraisal. And understand this is far different from the old, "Screw people—I don't care anything about them or what they think." This is simply about being free of ego-states that demand love or respect or obedience.

"We're advised to love our neighbors as we love ourselves. I cannot do otherwise, Dave. I will *always* do that. It's the only rule I can't break. I will love my neighbor as I love myself, meaning if I love myself, I'll be able to treat my neighbor with love; if I hate myself, I'll treat my neighbor with hatred. I'll *always* do it that way. If I can't get along with me, I darn sure can't get along with you. Even when you hear people repeating clichés instead of carrying the original message, I still have to love 'em or at least practice tolerance with them. Does that make sense, Dave?"

"How do I get there? This is driving me crazy."

"I've heard that statement somewhere before. Dave, have you ever been to New York?"

"Sure."

"Have you ever gone to the AT&T Building on Fifth Avenue?"

"No, can't say that I have."

"Let me tell you what I saw the last time I was there. It's something I've looked at dozens of times, but only after working all the steps was I really conscious of what I could learn. Standing in front of that building, I saw a character from mythology—Atlas—with the world on his shoulders. It's a terrible burden, having the world on your shoulders. Do you know that feeling, Dave?"

"Very well. I may be feeling it right now, in fact."

"So there he is with this huge world on his shoulders, troubled and laden. He's grimacing in many of the depictions of Atlas. But if you go across the street to St. Patrick's Cathedral, you can move to the front and see a carved hand. And do you know what's in that hand, Dave?"

"Nope."

"There's a tiny little world in that hand. You see, Dave, there's a Power of Consciousness—a Power of Perception or a Power that helps us see The Great Reality—that can take the world off our shoulders and reduce it down to proper proportion. The next time you go there, take that tour. Then, walk out of St. Patrick's and go to Rockefeller Center. It's a special place for alcoholics because the Rockefellers played an early role in the founding of our fellowship. In front of the building is a statue of Prometheus. He had displeased the gods, so they tied him up and let the vultures eat away at his liver. Can you relate to feeling 'tied up' and 'having something eat away at you,' Dave, especially at your liver?"

"Booze ate away at my liver for years. I'm right in the middle of this story. In fact, I *am* Prometheus. Go ahead."

"Well, one god, feeling compassion, freed him, unbound him, setting Prometheus loose and solving his liver problem as well. And you can see now in the face of that statue the delight of a man freed, flying off to a new and wonderful realm. And you can see him near that other character out of mythology with the world on his shoulders. Atlas? Or Prometheus? Those are your two options. The one we identify with depends on our thoughts and words and actions. If our thoughts and words and deeds are not in harmony, then the Body and Mind and Spirit and Emotions cannot be in harmony. The power of pure consciousness is the unifying element that brings into harmony all of the elements. Having the world on your shoulders...or having the world in your hands and being totally free? Which is it? That's what perspective can offer. That's the result of the regular contemplation and consideration that Mark and I practice. Your options now are to be bound up or unbound. Which shall it be, Dave? A call for action seems appropriate."

"What time do you do that meditation and contemplation and consideration work, Floyd?"

"7:00 A.M., every morning. See Dave, I'm only given enough power for today, and that's all I want. As an alcoholic, I wanted enough power for years; in fact, I want to be all-powerful. But I thrive in the discipline of getting my bread on a daily basis only. Having too much bread results in some of it spoiling—it spoils itself and it spoils me. So I have to get my bread daily. By the end of the day, ego-states could allow the world to make me feel bound up again. Today, my every need is met and no ego-states are in fear of not being enough or having enough. It seems to be a pretty good plan, actually."

"May I join you tomorrow?"

"I'll have the coffee on."

"I already feel as if something that's been binding me up is now being removed. See you tomorrow morning."

"MARK'S ANALYSIS OF
FLOYD'S BEHAVIOR—STEP ELEVEN"

Let me introduce a tool that leads to a state of higher consciousness. It's called the Eleventh Step. This step suggests an action that, when taken as specified, will improve and maintain conscious contact with the God of our understanding. All of the steps are ultimately experienced as states of consciousness, and each step builds upon all of the previous steps in a prescribed manner. By Step Nine, Floyd began to experience oneness with all people and all things. He subsequently entered into the World of the Spirit and began to be conscious and awake throughout the day, totally aware for the first time of what he is creating. Existing in this state, then, takes him to the daily discipline of Step Eleven.

Throughout the course of the day, he constantly shifts his thought-life when necessary in order to find truth and to be in contact with his True *SELF*. While his false selves were dominated by an array of liabilities, his True *SELF* is characterized by a list of wonderful assets. He begins to use the spiritual tools he has been given to change his thought-life and to allow those previously-hidden assets to emerge. He is now awake and aware of all that he is creating. His life takes on new meaning.

Finally, he begins to experience true peace inside himself, regardless of external conditions. His daily disciplines allow him to maintain fit spiritual condition and he will use them until he fixates in the complete and full awareness of Who He Really Is. If he continues to slide into ego-states, he must continue to use the tools of the Tenth and Eleventh Steps to see the *personas* and to be pulled away from those false states-of-being. With these thoughts in mind, we will now visit with Floyd to be certain that he understands all that the Eleventh Step requires of him if he is to maintain his recovered state of consciousness and to grow spiritually in order to maintain sanity.

"MARK GUIDES HIS PROTÉGÉ THROUGH STEP ELEVEN"

"Now, Floyd, it's time for us to talk about the tools that we will begin to use—if we so choose—to continue to improve our thought-life. Remember that we have an illness of body, mind, emotions and spirit. We have been taken to a state of consciousness that has resulted in our being recovered from our disease, a recovery that came about through our taking a series of actions involving the body, the mind, and the spirit. Having entered through the Tenth Step the World of the Spirit, meaning we have attained God-consciousness or Pure Consciousness, we will now pay closer attention to our thought-life as we create the type of life that we want to live."

"What do we have to do?"

"Upon awakening, we start the day by doing certain exercises that will divorce our thought-life from our self-will. We want to turn our thoughts immediately to the God of our understanding. Paying close attention to our thought-life, we ask for freedom from self-willed thoughts. We will also invite the new Power to guide and direct our thinking throughout the day. We will then go into a twenty or thirty-minute period of meditation. Remember, Floyd, that our goal is to be still. I asked you when we started this work what it means to 'be still.' You said it means 'Don't move.' Your answer was nowhere near correct. So let me ask you now, Floyd. What do you think it means to 'be still'?"

"Mark, I know exactly what it means now. It means I'm going to pause before reacting to anything. It means I will turn my thoughts and words and actions toward peace. I know now that instead of meaning 'don't move,' it really means 'move'—move away from chaos and move toward peace and love."

"Exactly, Floyd. You're going to be still so that you can allow the Pure Consciousness—which manifested in you after you began to be restored to sanity—to guide your thoughts in every instance during the entire course of the day. In the silence you might find that you begin to have certain images or visions come to you. The other action I take after coming out of the silence is to write. Write any thoughts that come to mind or write the details of your vision."

(Little could Floyd know that the vision he wrote would one day become a chapter in another book picked up by a publisher.)

Mark continued, "These writings will provide a way that you can form a journal of guidance received. After you look at the guidance objectively to test it to be certain that it is in alignment with what love would do, then proceed."

"Mark, your talk about 'being still' reminded me of something a friend told me about the British Navy. They deliver all their signals by way of a series of notes blown on a whistle, each series having its own name. He told me that in the direst emergencies they send forth a signal called 'Blowing the Still.' He asked me if I could guess what the seamen were trained to do when they heard an officer 'Blow the Still.' I said, 'I bet they run to their stations and prepare for battle,' but he said, 'Exactly the opposite, Floyd. It means, "You are facing a potentially calamitous emergency and you probably want to stiffen, to react, to become emotional and to prepare for a fight. Instead, be still, and hear the voice of your captain." That made me recall what you've taught me these last few weeks—that when I feel like I'm facing a dire emergency that in the past left me prone to go into battle-mode, I must do the opposite: I must be still and listen for the voice of love and peace and harmony to guide me."

"Floyd, you're finally getting it. You see, the payoff from this work is that we get to sit at one with All, to experience peace with All. Having done the work in the first ten steps, we have stilled our bodies and minds enough to allow us to experience true and lasting peace."

"This guidance I'm to seek is not different from what you read to me from the literature one night when you told me that I would develop a 'vital sixth sense,' right?"

"Precisely. You see, Floyd, it's from the state that results when we have tapped into the inner source—into that vital sense—that we go throughout the day knowing that we're being properly guided. The True *SELF* operates from the asset side of your personality, not from the liability side any longer. We turn time and again to our sixth sense, our intuition, which is just a natural resource that is within us that we are now conscious of. Before, you reacted from a state of unconsciousness. Now, you live deliberately, acting from a state of consciousness. Being awake and aware, you become conscious of the effects that your actions have on others and eventually on yourself. In that state, you stop putting out harm into the universe and you start behaving constructively. Remember, Floyd, we're trying to remember what we already know while trying to forget everything that we have learned—all of that wrong programming and faulty conditioning."

"You've helped me realize, Mark, that almost everything that I've learned—my belief systems about almost everything—have come from everywhere except inside of me. I suddenly understand why the literature told me to cast aside all ideas and emotions and attitudes. They were never *mine* to start with. Why should I hang onto them, and why should I let them hang onto me? They were the source of the wrong thinking and the overly-sensitive-feelings and the false beliefs that I adopted from others. None of that came intuitively from inside me."

"And so none of it was natural. None of it was the truth—the truth that your Real *SELF* knew from the beginning. Since I began practicing daily meditation in 1992, a complete change in my heart and in my mind has come about. I have a feeling of being guided, of being safe, of being protected even when I'm experiencing self-will—that is, 'fear.' You must consciously remind yourself that love, patience, and tolerance will begin to manifest through you in spite of yourself. You now have available spiritual tools to use as you go through the day, Floyd. Practice pausing. To pause is to use a great spiritual tool. When your thought-life or your emotions start to manifest through your behavior, pause and then turn. Turn to God...to Good. Ask before you act, 'What would Love do right now'?"

"Mark, I hear what you're saying, and I want the ability to do what you're suggesting. As far as I've come, I still don't know how close I am to being able to get where you are."

"Floyd, it can take time to develop the discipline to pause. It took you years to develop the habit of not pausing. You had the habit of reacting too quickly, so why expect that you can develop overnight the discipline to pause? Working with these spiritual tools is an awesome experience, Floyd. The use of these tools will alter your life. Being aware and awake and conscious of your thoughts, words, and deeds throughout the day will change your life. Ending your evening with a reflection on what you've created during the day and then entering into the stillness of meditation and contemplation for a few minutes—these actions will alter your life."

"Mark, I want what you have. I've got to get it into my brain that I can do this."

"Remember especially in Steps Two, Four, Five and Ten how we experienced entering into the World of the Mind—that is, into your thought-life?"

"Sure."

"Well remember, Floyd, your brain is not your mind. It is simply a tool, just as your leg or your arm is a tool. Be conscious of your thought-life. That's how you've touched The Great Reality that you now live in. If you don't like the reality in which you live, don't blame anyone or anything else, for it is you who creates that reality."

"Now I see. That's what you meant when you said that all of my troubles...."

"...were of your own making. All of our troubles are always of our own making."

"You make holding onto what I have sound easy."

"Easy, Floyd, except for the fact that you must be the one to set the alarm clock. You're the one who must choose to take the actions that will produce the discipline. I once asked you what there was before there was everything and you couldn't imagine what I meant. Can you imagine what I mean now?"

"Of course, Mark. There was *nothing*."

"Right, Floyd—there was nothing indeed. Now, think of your drinking days. What was there before the journey through all twelve steps re-created everything in your life?"

"There was nothing, Mark, nothing except chaos. My life was

null and void."

"Right. You've moved off the stage of the Theater of the Lie where you were playing all those phony roles. In doing so, you entered into conscious awareness of Who You Really Are. You spoke of 'returning home' earlier. This is called 'coming home,' Floyd, coming home to your True *SELF*. You have taken a twelve-step journey to *SELF*-transformation, to being transformed from one who was asleep and being driven by his false ego-states to identifying with your one True *SELF*. That removes the insanity of the schizophrenic life you were living with multiple identities that were all false. Floyd's *perception* of 'Who He Is' has been transformed from *thinking* that he was all those phony roles he played to *knowing* Who He Really Is. Your mind has been transformed in a way that makes your past liabilities anathema and makes your previously-hidden assets something quite appealing. Those pushy and controlling liabilities that your ego-states in their fear took to be tools of strength you now see were really nothing more than the blustering of a fearful child inside. You can now behave as a confident adult since you are at one with your True *SELF*, with a newly-found Power, with Pure Consciousness and sanity...with All. And in the process of under-going 'A Twelve Step Journey to *SELF*-Transformation,' you have been transformed from a creator of chaos into a creator of peace...in yourself and in others. Enjoy, Brother."

"Thank you, Mark."

"Passing It On"

"You see, Danny," Floyd said into the telephone, "we need to know if you're willing to go to any length to recover from a hopeless state of body, mind, emotions and spirit. Secondly, we need to know if you're willing to take the necessary action to undergo a complete change of heart and mind. Are you?"

"Yeah, Floyd. I am. So what do I have to do?"

"Well, Danny, what you have to do is have an *experience* with Step One. You're going to have to experience that you are powerless over alcohol and that your life is unmanageable."

"Oh, Floyd, I know that already."

"Danny, if *knowledge* of what is wrong with you would help, we wouldn't be having this discussion. You must *experience* your hopelessness to receive hope; you must *experience* your powerlessness to receive power; you must *experience* your insanity to receive sanity."

"Floyd, that makes no sense at all."

"Neither did all those years of drinking and the subsequent consequences, but you did it, anyway. So that's why we're going to go ahead and do this work now, if you're willing. You see, Danny, the spiritual life is about your remembering what you already know in your heart and 'unlearning' everything in your wrongly-programmed mind that you've been taught. You don't need *more* programming or *re*-programming. I'd be a complete egomaniac to suggest that I am the one who knows how your mind should be reprogrammed. But what my experience with my own mind showed is that we do need *de*-programming. You need to undergo a process that will allow you to cast aside ideas, emotions, and attitudes which have locked you into a state of self-will and thus chaos. And though your false ego-states will want to fight for their identities that are rooted in your wrong beliefs, you might become willing to give them up if you see that those states aren't truly You and that your beliefs were never *yours* to begin with.

"The bottom line is this: if there isn't a complete change in your ideas, your thought-life, your emotions, and your attitudes, you will never recover and you will be doomed to die an alcoholic death. Even before that death, you'll be doomed to live a miserable alcoholic life...whether drunk or sober. The dry drunk days for me were as miserable as the wet drunk days. The only thing worse than feeling the way I felt when I was drinking was feeling that same way *without* drinking—without something to drown out the misery. I can guide you to a solution that differs from both those states. The path of trying to live by self-will is the path to misery and death. If you want to live on a different basis, then we'll go through the Twelve Steps together and you'll experience each one of them. Then you'll automatically begin to live naturally, harming no one and no thing, including yourself.

"That sounds hopeless. It's too much."

"Well, you see, Danny, the paradox is this: the more helpless you feel, the better it will be. All your life, Brother, you've had one of those talking alarm clocks. You woke up every morning with it shouting: '*Are...you...ready...to...rumble?!*' I'm asking, 'Are you ready to humble?' Are you ready to humble yourself and surrender to the process of going through certain steps, admitting that maybe you don't know everything and that maybe there are some new things that can benefit you if you put forth the effort to experience them?

"See, you've always been Rocky. You get up in the morning playing 'Danny the Real Man,' eating raw eggs and ready to fight. You race through the streets; you're trying to climb to the highest point in the city; you're raising your fist into the air in defiance and you're shaking it at all the world. And in the end, you declare victory. Your arm is raised in triumph. But guess what, Danny. At the end of the day, you're more beat up than the one you claim to have defeated. You think that's a victory? You fought the war of life, Danny, and you lost. You took on the world: *'Today, in this very arena, the feature attraction—Danny versus...everyone!'* To fight with those odds is insane. We can give up—we can surrender. We can call off the fight, but since that runs counter to everything in the alcoholic's very being, we have to get help to call off the fight. That takes *real* power. In here, we get connected with that real Power."

"Floyd, I've had some people at different meetings telling me to take it easy, to go slow. This seems like you're moving too fast according to what I've been told."

"OK, let's forget for a moment that the founders did the steps with newcomers in four hours or less and then guided them to additional sources for additional treatment for what ailed them. I'll try it this way, telling you a story, Danny. Its content is fiction but its truth is real. Supposedly, after the fellowship began, the alcohol manufacturers and distributors called a meeting of the best advisors from across the globe. They were losing too many of their customers in the early days of the program. They decided that they had to send their henchmen out to infiltrate and to spread around ideas that might lead us back to the damnation of a life of pure hell, both now and forevermore.

"The first advisor said, 'Let's go into their meetings and sit at their tables and tell them over and over, "Just don't drink and go to meetings." If we can get them to spread that around, that'll guarantee they fail.' And the chairman of the world's largest distributor of alcoholic beverages said, 'Nope, surely deep inside they know that there's got to be more required than that to heal their bodies and spirits and minds, and there's huge numbers who have gone back out who are testifying to the fact that it takes more than sitting in a meeting to address everything that needs addressing. I can't possibly imagine that would get them.'

"A second advisor said, 'How about if we tell them that in this crazy world there's no chance for hope or for peace and that they may as well give up and go drink to find a little escape from a tough world'? The corporate executive said, 'That won't work because they've seen the ones who were hopeless before but found new, long-term hope after doing all the steps, so surely they'd never go for that.'

"Disgusted with what he took to be ideas that surely not even a drunk would ever buy into, the executive called for his most devious, most cunning, most baffling advisor. He moved forward out of the shadows in the back. His appearance was so hideous that the other advisors were forced to look down at their feet. He smelled of venom and hatred. He was Evil personified. When he spoke, his breath was so foul that even the rotten chief executive had to grimace and turn his head. But when he shared the words of his plan, all in that boardroom who heard his proposal *knew* that he had, indeed, come up with the strategy that would destroy all *real alcoholics* who would ever begin seeking recovery.

"He opened his despicable mouth and he said in a slow, staccato delivery that echoed throughout the chamber of the boardroom: 'Tell them…that they have…plenty of time!' And all of the advisors joined the director and shouted, 'That's it! That'll do it! Tell them not to rush into anything—to take it slow and easy!' And you know what, Danny. They were right. If you're a *real alcoholic* and believe that you have plenty of time and you decide to seek recovery in a slow and easy fashion, you'll stay miserable or you'll die. You and I can go out and take the first drink tonight, and we can die. Or we can do what huge numbers have done—the ones who killed themselves in the misery of giving up the booze but not giving up the wrong thinking and painful feelings that made it seem necessary in the first place. Danny, we *real alcoholics* don't have plenty of time."

"Floyd, none of this makes sense, but you're right: neither did all those years of drinking."

"See, Danny, in Greek there are two words for 'time.' One is *chronos*. That's time measured by clocks and calendars. Then there's *kairos*. *Kairos* is a moment of true, universal consciousness in time.

Actually, it's not even in time—it's simply that moment known as 'now,' which is the only real 'time' there is. *Kairos* can manifest itself in relationship to a problem that can then be transformed into an opportunity. *Kairos* is one of those brief and fleeting flashes of 'now-ness' when opportunity can manifest itself to eliminate a life-long problem. It's that moment—that 'right now' second—when the chance comes along to shift into a condition of becoming awake, aware, and conscious. The *kairos* moment is that moment that comes in this relative existence that represents a micro-second of opportunity to be free of all the horror in your past and present and to eliminate all insane, self-destructive behaviors from your future. It is that moment that presents itself so that one can regain sanity and get free of all the wrong programming and faulty conditioning and then come into contact with Who You Really Are.

"Danny, right *now* may be your *kairos* moment. This moment may be the one in which you make the decision to begin a course of action that will make the supernatural in your life become the natural. It is a process that Mark taught me which I can now pass on to you. You have a thought-life that's killing you. We can begin to change it *now*. You have a word-life that's killing you. We can begin to change it *now*. You have a deed-life that's killing you. We can begin to change it *now*. Those are only invitations, but if you're a *real alcoholic*, you may not have a lot of *chronos* left, pal. The only thing you may have left is *kairos*. So, Danny, what's it going to be? *Chronos*? Or *kairos*?"

"I want to grab the moment, Floyd. I want a chance. Let's go."

"Good, we'll meet tonight at my place at 8:00. See you then."

"Hey, Floyd."

"Yeah."

"Thanks. I don't know why, but I suddenly feel like there might be an answer to my dilemma, that there might finally be hope. It's like alcohol has had me bound up all my life, but in this moment, I feel like the bindings are loosened a bit."

"See you tonight, Danny."

As soon as Floyd replaced the telephone into the cradle, the phone rang. "Hello."

"Hey, Bro. It's Mark."

"Mark. What are you doing?"

"Talking to you."

"I just got off the phone with my first prospect after going through all of The Work with you."

"How'd it go?"

"Well, we're only getting started, but it all came back to me. Everything you showed me, I was able to pass it on in order to get a commitment from him. And going through only as much as I did with him just now, I really felt my original hopelessness, my original powerlessness, my original insanity. And then I felt all of the wonder and joy of my new consciousness and awareness and sanity. I felt useful, really useful, for the first time in my life. I want to tell you what this guy said. As I was sharing, he said, 'This makes no sense at all.' [Laughing] Remember when I said that?"

"Yeah, that was yesterday, wasn't it?"

"Don't push it, mister."

"Floyd, what's important is that *you* remember when you said that. Never forget those days when you spoke so insanely. Never forget the thought-life you lived in that made you say that. It will give you the compassion that you'll need to help others, and it'll remind you of where you've been and where we could go again."

"You got that right, Mark. So can we get together and discuss the Twelfth Step before I meet with Danny at 8:00 tonight?"

"Be here at 6:00"

"See you then. Bye."

"Bye."

"Mark Explains the Final Stage of Preparing His Protégé for Twelfth Step Work"

The actions taken by the alcoholic in the first eleven steps transform a man or woman from a person who could not quit drinking—regardless of good reasons or bad consequences—and delivered that alcoholic from the suffering associated with his or her multi-tiered disease. More exactly, the alcoholic has been delivered into an experiencing—and then a personal knowing of—a power and a resource from within. That experience moves the alcoholic from an unconscious state of mind, body and spirit into a state of recovery in which the alcoholic enjoys an awakened body, an awakened mind, an awakened spirit. The alcoholic has undergone a profound change in his thought-life from which all of his actions arise, and he will now be a different person in terms of conscious thoughts. Also, the experience is the beginning of a shift toward freedom from emotional intoxication which results when all necessary action is taken to do what the literature suggests—namely, cast aside ideas, emotions, and attitudes.

With the change in his thought-life has come a sweeping change in his words and actions. He has begun to re-create his life. Now, the recovered alcoholic has begun to experience his true oneness with all things, with all people, and with his new-found Power. He no longer feels apart and separated; he no longer feels "dis-ease." Moving into the twelfth step, he or she will begin to be of service to others. He will reach out to other alcoholics who are in the same horrible position in life that the recovered alcoholic was once in, and he will offer hope to the suffering alcoholic. Life for the alcoholic in recovery will now have a purpose. He will help to unbind others. He will escort them along the path of their own journey to *SELF*-transformation.

Alcoholics in recovery will become "at one" with all and they will have a clear intent to be helpful rather than destructive. Their sense of having been restored to sanity will produce within their heart a deep longing to help others who are much like themselves. They will be willing to go anywhere at any time to help their fellow traveler on the journey. From the ashes of the bitter past has risen a life that has literally become a gushing stream of love, acceptance, gratitude and peace. Recovered alcoholics can now transmit their experience to others, and they will begin to experience life in the Fellowship of the Spirit. Notice, please, that the miracle of change came as quickly to Floyd as he worked the steps. The steps can be completed in a short time, for we never underestimate the Power that can bring about change quickly, though it can only come as fast as one is willing to complete the step work.

As Floyd told Danny, *real alcoholics* don't have the unlimited time to seek recovery that they are sometimes led to believe.

With these thoughts in mind, I'll meet with Floyd in final preparation for him to begin to seek out other alcoholics who are suffering in order to carry this message and to pass on to them what has been given to him.

"Mark Explains Twelfth Step Work to His Protégé"

"Floyd, this will be our last talk for a while. From the beginning of this relationship, I have consistently told you that recovery from alcoholism is about your experiencing and knowing a God of your own conception. The series of actions that you took through the first eleven steps have prepared you now to be of service to others, and that doesn't mean alcoholics only. You will begin to truly experience the truth of 'love your neighbors as you love yourself'."

"Well, Mark, I'm certainly excited about working with Danny and others and taking them on this journey. But I'm not totally confident, what with all the responsibility that this implies. I'd like some guidelines, if you have any ideas."

"Floyd, there are two spiritual laws that I always follow when working with others. Let's review those before you go out to work with others. The first is the Law of Consent: if a person does not give me consent to help, then I am intruding and I have no right to do that. Protégés can still be belligerent or argumentative even though they've come to me for help. I have to see that they're willing and that they fully consent to the process if we're to move on. The second law I follow is the Law of Caring. If your actions show that you don't care about working at your spiritual growth and about seeking a spiritual experience that will restore you to sanity, then I cannot—and I will not—help. With these two laws in effect, Floyd, I suggest that you sit down with an alcoholic and go through the literature section on the steps. Whenever the literature says to do something, you do it. That's pretty simple, isn't it?"

"Yep."

"Good, Floyd! A simple, one-word answer! I'm in shock! You really are getting better."

Floyd twisted his lips, but the look he gave Mark was not one of those "I-wish-this-look-could-bring-about-your-demise-this-instant" type looks that he arrogantly gave to Mark in the early going when Floyd heard some truth that his ego could not accept. Mark laughed and went on. "Remember that you're to show those you work with exactly what has happened to you through following a specific course of action. That's what helping others is all about, Floyd, and remember that you are to be kind, loving, self-sacrificing and tolerant. The rest will happen."

"I'm glad I never did or said anything while you were carrying me through The Work that tested your patience or made you have to practice tolerance!"

"You're pushing it, again, Floyd, but I'm glad to see that you can laugh at your old false self now. Maybe you've learned what I was trying to share with you about being too sensitive. Also, don't concern yourself with the approval of others. If I seek your approval, I become your prisoner. The truth will always be revealed to us from the inside, not from anybody or anything on the outside. Spend time with people who are seeking truth through a specific course of action. Take a look at the places you visit; notice who you're spending your time with. Being around negative energy which has no desire to find positive energy can be crippling. Be conscious, awake, and aware. Now, Floyd, tell me again what it means to 'be sober'."

"You've shown me that 'being sober' means being conscious, aware, and awake. It's being aware of my Real *SELF* and my assets."

"Very good, Floyd. And what's the advantage to your being sober, that is, conscious, aware, and awake?"

"The advantage to me is, since I reap what I sow, I need to be very aware at all times so that I know what I'm sowing. Since I'm sowing constantly, either by thought, word, or deed, I need to be conscious of what I'm creating at all times. No more firing off of the mouth unconsciously. We have to be conscious of everything we think and say and do. We are now to be of maximum service to others and to the True *SELF* that we have always been. Aligned with the Power, we will discover ourselves being consciously involved with what we are creating, with being responsible, with seeking guidance and strength."

"Very good, Floyd. And we'll pay attention to our thought-life, our word-life, and our deed-life. We can now commence with making a life that is happy, joyous, and free. You can operate from a state called 'Love' and—from that state—peace and joy and freedom must follow. Sounds like you have something real to share with Danny tonight. Now go, and pass it on."

"Thanks, Mark."

"No…thank you."

CHAPTER 18

"LIFE AFTERWARDS: I AM AWAKENED"

After working the steps with Mark and receiving many major benefits, I remained grateful that he appeared in my life when he did. I had said that *scientists speak of parallel universes and geometry talks of parallel lines—lines running an equal distance apart at all points and never touching. Sometimes there are distant lives that seem to run a parallel course. Occasionally...they just happen to touch.* Fortunately for me, our lives just happened to touch. As we did The Work together, we wrote. This book is the product of that experience.

Months later, in a room above a sanctuary where I would soon be introducing him to a crowd that was gathering below—a crowd to whom he would be carrying the message—Mark took from his pocket and handed me the special Vietnam Veterans Recovery Medallion that he had used for years during his morning prayer and meditation time. Before he hugged me, he put into my hand that chip. Then he looked me in the eyes and he said, "Happy Eighth Birthday! You made it! Now get out of here. I need a period of quiet before I speak to the people downstairs." I walked outside, shut the door, stopped in the hall and looked down at the chip in my hand.

Some strange, powerful, not-of-this-world-feeling washed over me, and it seemed as if I heard a voice coming from inside the room I had just left, a voice that was not Mark's (though booming Mark's voice surely is). No, this was as if I heard some other powerful voice in that room speak and say:

"WELL DONE, MY GOOD AND FAITHFUL SERVANT. I WILL CONTINUE TO BRING THEM BACK FROM DEATH INTO LIFE. YOU CONTINUE TO UNBIND THEM . . . AND SET THEM FREE."

But then, it seemed that the voice was not an actual, vocal voice. It seemed more like something I was sensing with some vital sense I now had. Then I realized that the voice was not coming from inside that room at all but seemed to be coming from somewhere deep inside me. A nagging feeling came as I knew that there were some things Mark had told me when working the steps that would explain what I was experiencing, but I couldn't bring them into consciousness. I determined that the next morning I would spend all the time required in consideration and contemplation until the understanding of all that had just happened was revealed to me.

The next morning in the quiet, all that had happened was revealed to Floyd.

*

PART TWO

THE MENTAL

*

CHAPTER 19

"THE AFTERMATH"

While we divided our book into parts to share our experiences in seeking the four levels of healing and sobriety discussed by Bill W., we found that no real divisions exist. All in this manifestation, we discovered in our case, is but one whole. That required for us a holistic treatment approach to bring about healing and to give us all four levels of sobriety.—Mark and Floyd

In the years following Mark's step work with Floyd, Mark continued to work the steps with alcoholics, taking thousands through the process. Floyd helped organize groups that worked the steps and also took thousands of alcoholics through the twelve steps.

Their experiences, which have come through working with such large numbers of people seeking recovery, made clear to them that step work completed in the fashion described in the first part of this book was all that some problem drinkers needed. Their observations and experiences also support the truth of what is revealed in the literature: that step work was part of the overall treatment plan used by the founders to guide some protégés to recovery but that it was often just one of the many important elements in the founders' overall treatment plan for *real alcoholics*.

How does one know—once one has done the step work and continues with inventory, meditation and service work—if she/he is "done" or if more is required? How does one know if he/she has gained all necessary to live a sane and normal and happy and joyous and free life? How does one know if a need exists to explore what the literature predicted when it says that "more will be disclosed"? How does one know if step work alone is all he needs or if he needs to find out what else had *been disclosed* in the many decades since that line was written? Eventually, both Floyd and Mark would find that more *became disclosed* to them and that they did indeed need more. They would allow the literature to guide them in traveling along those additional avenues, and in this book they will reveal "The Other Steps" they had to take.

CHAPTER *20*

"ARE YOU DONE?"

Some people might find that undergoing the process described in the step work detailed in *Part One* of this book, *The Spiritual*, is sufficient for total recovery in all four areas mentioned by Bill W. Some might be like Mark and me and find they weren't done. What accounts for the difference? "Moderate drinkers" and "hard drinkers," we are told, can quit when they are presented with evidence that drinking is not working for them. Such advice as "just don't drink" can actually be effective with them because exposure to the fact that drinking is not working for them is often enough. Similarly, for others burdened only with certain personality disorders, step work can lead to the desired shift in behavior. The literature makes clear that those types of moderate or hard drinkers do not have the grave emotional and mental disorders or the major body damage that often plague *real alcoholics*.

If a *real alcoholic* tries to recover a sound body and mind and spirit by using only the methods that were effective for moderate or hard drinkers, Bill W. made clear that the alcoholic is most likely going to fail. So the answer we found to the question, "Are You Done?" is "That depends."

If a drinking problem is rooted in a personality disorder and one had an awakening after reading the details of Floyd's experience as Mark guided him through the step work, that type person might be done. For others like Mark and Floyd, more is required. The literature points out that even with *real alcoholics*, the founders took only four hours or less to work the steps to provide a "spiritual experience" and to begin the shift toward a "spiritual awakening." In that short matter of hours, drinkers recognized what the founders wanted them to see via step work: that a name for their "ailment" exists; that they don't drink like normal drinkers; that they can never drink normally; that their past behaviors were not working for them; that they have some relationship repairing to do…with others, with their bodies, with their minds; that they must take more action to "cast aside ideas, emotions, and attitudes" in order to be *de*-programmed and emotionally sober; and that they might need to pursue additional assistance in the future from professionals.

Often, the wakeup call that came from step work was the eye-opener, the great beginning for *real alcoholics*. Afterwards, the founders often directed their protégés to trained specialists in various fields. The identity of those trained professionals that the founders often referred their members is revealed in the literature as a group of "doctors, psychologists and practitioners of various kinds." The goal of using such outside help was to provide specific treatment for the emotions, the body, and the mind, if needed.

The founders usually hospitalized their prospects for several days at the beginning of the process, using chemicals to detox their newcomers. Their original plan called for creation of a worldwide network of treatment center-hospitals. The original vision included admitting <u>every</u> *real alcoholic* for medical treatment prior to beginning step work and for follow-up work afterwards, guided by professionally-trained doctors, psychologists, psychiatrists, and nutritionists. Having seen that some moderate and hard drinkers do not need such extensive and continuing assistance, we focus on the needs of the *real alcoholics* and ask, "When is more assistance required?"

"OUR ADDITIONAL NEEDS"

Mark and I have each taken thousands of alcoholics through the steps and have often observed the long-term results of that step work on protégés. We also both *experienced* first-hand the wisdom of the founders when they identified different types of drinkers and used different courses of action for treating the different types who came to the fellowship for help. It became obvious, in our own cases, that we both needed for *more to be disclosed* as promised. The experiences of many others whom we worked with demonstrated the same. Beyond the step work treatment for the addictive personality and the personality disorders that we suffered, Mark and I both eventually had to admit that we also needed specific, specialized treatment for the emotional and mental and physical aspects of our illness that the literature makes references to. We shall offer what we observed from our own experiences and from working with other *real alcoholics*. Mark will share what we experienced.

CHAPTER 21

"MARK'S REALIZATION:
'I NEEDED MORE'"

Belief systems can be one of the greatest barriers to freedom from self that we will ever encounter. As my own experience now shows, I found it necessary to pursue several courses of action in addition to what Floyd and I have discussed in the step work portion entitled "Part One: The Spiritual." The areas that needed more work and additional assistance include family of origin work; trauma and post-traumatic-stress-disorder therapy; nutritional guidance; help with my nicotine addiction; and further treatment of the addictive personality. At one time I had a belief system that the steps alone would be enough. That belief system almost killed me.

I do not pretend to have answers for any other person, but my own experience motivates me to encourage people to look at their own experience and to ask two questions: "How is that working?" and "Do I have a sense that I could benefit from more assistance in some areas?" The answers can help one see if additional courses of action are required to attain that peace that we all deserve.

I have explored meditation for years and still have a daily practice; I have visited many monasteries; I have read many books by many different spiritual teachers of all religions and all of it has contributed to enriching my life; nevertheless, an analysis of the functioning of my physical body's organs and my emotional and mental states revealed that much corrective action was needed even after all of the step work and all of the spiritual work that I did. I gained the additional treatment needed through nutritional supplements (as recommended by a doctor, not selected by me) as well as through exercise, therapy, and modifications to my food plan.

The benefits I have derived over the past two years from taking "The Other Steps" to seek the additional help referenced in the literature are difficult to describe. They have contributed to a greater restoration of sanity for me. I have sought financial counsel and was encouraged to look at the belief systems I had been taught to see how ineffective they were and to commit to changes in my monetary life. All of these additional courses of action have allowed me to grow more and more into a state of sanity not attained before; into a state of deeper peace not attained before; into greater awareness and into a greater state of authenticity not attained before. Again, I have no desire to tell anyone what they should or should not do, but I suggest that all can let their own inner intuition be a guide to determine if a new path or further aid should be considered.

I urge all to be careful about listening to individuals who want to enlist you to accept and to follow their belief systems. Your own experience will always be your best guide, but I suggest combining that with a seeking of counsel from additional professionals and experts in varied fields, just as the literature discusses. My own experience inspires me to suggest to all that we be open-minded and consider new possibilities beyond those limited to one path. I recommend that all trust that Intuitive Force within and then, most of all, "To thine own *SELF* be true."

CHAPTER 22

"WHY DON'T YOU CHOOSE YOUR OWN CONCEPTION OF GOD?"

After having my experience through doing the step work with Mark, many began coming my way. Many responded well to the approach I used that was modeled upon the method used in "Part One" of this book; however, along with them came a large population of people explaining that they were having trouble with "the God Part." When they showed up in my life and I tried to use with them the same method that Mark used with me, they failed to make it through the steps with that approach. I went back to the literature to seek what I needed to help that segment in the fellowship as well.

Ultimately, what I got into touch with via working the steps with Mark was The Great Reality. I suffered all my life under the influence of The Great Delusion, the delusional thinking that results from wrong programming and faulty conditioning. To reach that state of seeing reality, the notion of a resource located within resonates with some. For others I worked with, I saw them responding to a concept of an inner, intuitive power—that "vital sixth sense." The term "Universal Mind" made sense to some alcoholics trying to be rid of their wrong-thinking mind. Since the open-minded people in the fellowship were willing to allow me the benefit of my own conception of the Power of the universe, today I gladly tolerate others' concepts without questioning them in the least. Thank goodness that, in my case, Mark was willing to say: *I see that certain abuses that you have suffered—and still suffer— have left you recoiling from some concepts associated with them. How about if we use a concept of a power that is not gender specific or God specific? Where I use 'Him' and 'He' and 'God,' I could as easily use 'Her' or 'She' or 'Goddess' or any other terms offered in the literature to point toward that Higher Power required for recovery.*

As I worked with more alcoholics, I found that those among the indigenous peoples responded to the concept of a "Spirit of Nature." For others with an Eastern bent, "Prime Cause" seemed to make step work more accessible to them. My experience has shown the validity of the literature's recommendation that we be willingness to allow those in our fellowship to "choose their own conception of God." I have watched people work the steps with me who have a wide variety of concept about the Power, and they still gain a full and complete spiritual experience and awakening.

I appreciate the fact that Mark—and other open-minded people who eventually offered assistance to me—allowed me the right to conceive in my own fashion whatever power we discussed, just as the literature suggests. My concept today might vary considerably from Mark's concept, and that's OK. Certain past experiences and certain on-going experiences when I met Mark would have closed me off to receiving any additional help if I had been forced to accept exactly another person's concept of God.

So now, our readers have a choice. We have provided two guides, two *ways*, if you will. The following guide is useful for those who have worked the steps in a traditional fashion the way that Mark modeled with me but who are now looking for additional help in getting a new mindset, in improving their thinking, or in getting more help in the areas of what the literature calls our "grave *emotional* and *mental*" problems; thus, the guide is a way to have a "working-the-steps experience" that focuses on improving both the mental and the emotional state. It is also a guide that helps people get started in sponsoring and taking people through the steps since it can be used verbatim in the beginning until sponsors find their own literature-based way to guide their protégés.

The guide that follows will also work with *anyone* with an addictive personality, no matter their concept of God. The method varies somewhat from the way Mark took me through the steps as depicted in the early chapters in this book but has proved no less effective. Also, a sponsor can use the guide and insert a traditional concept of God if he prefers and if the protégé prefers. We are not trying to tell anyone how to do anything.

The guide has been used by hundreds to take thousands through the steps. In one form or another over the years, we have been told that it has been translated for use in Sweden, Spain, Canada, Mexico, Finland, Israel, Iceland, and more than half of the U.S. states. Just as experience showed us that the method Mark used with me really works, so experience shows the same about this method as well. Whether one uses the model that Mark used with me in "Part One" or whether one uses the slightly different approach in the guide that follows, both methods presented are ultimately based in information offered in the literature, and both methods have been proven effective with the variety of people who have come to us for help.

A Guide for Working the Steps

*A Guide for *Sponsors*
* A Guide for Helping with *Emotional* and *Mental* Needs
*A Guide for Helping those with a *Traditional View of God*
or
*Even for Helping Those Claiming Trouble with *"the God Part"*

RATIONALE OF THE GUIDE

This guide was written after interviewing people who worked the steps with the founders and shared with us the way that some founders guided them through the steps in the early days when the success rates for recovery were so much higher than typical rates today. The guide also is based on information collected from people who were taken through the steps by Dr. Bob and by Clarence S. as well as from information shared by Clarence S. in interviews and while face-to-face with a member of one of Floyd's home groups. That being said, *we are not trying to tell anyone how to do anything.* We are sharing our experience with something that has helped some who needed more help.

This guide was first written <u>in response to requests</u> from people who recovered, and recovered quickly, as a result of working the steps in the way outlined here. Floyd used the method orally for years and then people asked him to write out what he and others were sharing in the process so they would have a guide for helping themselves and for helping others. You may first want to use the guide yourself. Then, in your twelfth-step work with others, you may want to use this guide one-on-one with another in the recovery process, reading it to a protégé page-by-page. If you prefer the way Mark took me through the steps instead, the first section is available as a guide.

The guide is divided into four parts which take an hour or so each, the inventory section often running a little longer. Many say, "That's impossible," but that's the timeframe that many of the founders used. While we had doubts, we tried it and it worked! Mark's method with me in "Part One" took a few hours more because of scheduling and geographic restrictions, but only a matter of hours were required with that approach as well. As Mark tells us, "This process need not be long and arduous."

Your protégés can benefit from having their own copy of the book since they'll do their writing in *The Workbook* and their at-home reading in the *Appendix* and will then also have a guide for helping others. (Websites for ordering appear in Chapter 28.) You can have your protégé commit to a particular day or night of the week for four weeks, or you can schedule the entire process in one day or over a matter of weeks as Mark did with me. The plan allows flexibility so all schedules can be accommodated. We have seen this guide work when you read it *with* protégés or *to* protégés, always waiting for their answers to the questions. Later, you'll have the method down and can "wing it" on your own, modifying and using what you find to be most effective with your protégés and your style in particular. We are seeking to guide protégés to having an *experience* that results in an awakening, and that can come about in many ways. Best regards in helping yourself and others.

STEP MEETING ONE

(TO COVER STEPS ONE, TWO AND THREE)

[Sponsor/Leader says]: Bill Wilson said once in a lead talk that the *teaching* and *practicing* of the Twelve Steps is the *only* purpose of any recovery group, so our journey through the steps will focus on his statement. In order to help accomplish that goal, we have a guide that has a proven record with three groups: (1) those who hold a traditional view of God (note to sponsors: in the guide, simply insert the name "God" wherever you choose); (2) those who have worked the steps but sense they could benefit from further assistance with the *mental* and *emotional* aspects of the illness; and (3) those alcoholics who claim to have a problem working the steps because they need to be given the offer made in the literature to form their own conception of a Higher Power, even it is differs from the traditional.

The approach is interactive, so we'll be asking some questions throughout which we'll invite you to answer. First, do you want to *1.* find a design for living that is better than what you've had, drunk or not drunk? (Wait for answer.)

The percentages who try to stop drinking but go back out are high. Some founders noted that those who went back out usually stopped the step work either after Step Three or after Step Eight. *2* So, are you willing to take *all twelve* steps required for successful completion? (Answer) (A) How soon do you want to get better? (Answer) (B) Then let's see which type drinker you are. Two types, moderate and hard drinkers, can quit on their own if they have a good reason. The third type doesn't quit, even with many good reasons indicated. Only two things make one the third type, which is the *real alcoholic*: we lost choice and we lost control. Did you ever say you were going to quit, then tried to quit but didn't? (Answer) Then you lost choice. Did you ever say you were going to drink but were going to control the amount you drank, but failed? (Answer) Then you lost control. So, do you concede to your innermost self that you are not a moderate or hard drinker but that you are a *real alcoholic*? (Answer)

There is a need to work the steps if a life has any of the eight traits of untreated alcoholism. Can you relate to any of these? 1. We had trouble in personal relationships, including with ourselves, at work, in traffic, etc. (Answer) 2. We couldn't control our emotional natures. Do you ever have up and down days? Have you ever behaved irrationally because of fears or for love? (Answer) 3. We were a prey to misery and depression (Answer) 4. We couldn't make a living—a decent life (Answer) 5. We felt useless—or very useful—but knew deep down inside that we weren't. (Answer) 6. We felt full of fear—we worried a lot (Answer) 7. We were unhappy (Answer) 8. We couldn't be of real help to other people (Answer). So have you experienced one or more of those? (Answer) Then it's time to work the steps.

STEP ONE has two parts. It says: **We admitted that we were powerless over alcohol—that our lives had become unmanageable.** "Powerless" over alcohol means we lost choice and lost control. We'll explain why later. An "unmanageable life" means that life is crazy or that we don't feel happy, joyous, or free. We do crazy things when we're drinking, but we do crazy things when we're not drinking, too. Do you agree that a crazy, unhappy life is a poorly managed life? (Answer) Do you want to find out how to change that? (Answer)

Alcoholism is an illness which includes an allergy of the body and an obsession of the mind. The first part is physical. We are powerless over alcohol physically. Why? Are you allergic to a food or a medicine, or can you name something you hate to eat? (*Ex.: avocado*) What effect does it have on you? (Ex.: *Avocado makes me throw up.*) So you've never had any (*Ex.: avocado—fill-in-the-blank with their answer given*) since finding out the effect?

(Answer) What effect did alcohol have on you at the end of your drinking experience? (Answer) So you can control your consumption of (*Ex.: avocado*) because it does this (*fill-in-the-blank with the effect the protégé named*), but you can't do the same with alcohol. Here's why. There is something called "the phenomenon of craving" that alcoholics suffer. We'll use the abbreviated name of one component that alcohol breaks down into after consumption. It's called "acetate," and that's a chemical that passes through the liver and pancreas. It has been identified as the chemical that triggers a craving for another drink. In many people, the acetate is broken down and passed on quickly, so those people have never experienced what it is like to crave a drink. Alcoholics have a liver and a pancreas that typically function at a less-than-normal rate, often slowing even more as we grow older. Because the liver and pancreas of an alcoholic function slower, the acetate stays in us, creating a craving for another drink. We have another. Now we have two times the craving. Then we take a third drink and we have a craving three times stronger than any normal drinker can experience. We usually cannot stop after that "allergy" kicks in. Have you ever experienced that phenomenon of craving? (Answer) Then do you concede to your innermost self that this allergy, this phenomenon of craving, makes you physically powerless over alcohol and that you can never change that physical allergy and that it is only going to get progressively worse as you grow older? (Answer)

Next, the second part of our disorder is mental. Why? You have an effective mental defense against (*Ex. Avocado—fill-in-the-blank*). You stopped consuming it after you experienced the ill effects. But you keep going back to alcohol, even after having experienced many negative effects. Here's why. All people have the *conscious* part of the mind which determines what we *say*, and the *subconscious* part which often really determines what we *do* and how we *feel*. For example, with our conscious minds we'd say, "I'll never do *that* again," but we did. Why? Because of what's in the subconscious mind and because of the fact that the subconscious mind influences us more powerfully than the conscious mind. Some call the conscious mind the physical mind. Illogical behavior comes from the subconscious mind. Here's an example: One of our members, when a child, suffered twenty-six wasp stings to the head. Today, in his 50's, if a fly buzzes by his ear, he jumps. Is it normal to jump if a fly goes by? No. Does he understand why he jumps? Yes. He knows that somewhere in his subconscious mind is a record of the pain he suffered five decades earlier. But even understanding that does not stop his abnormal reaction. **Knowledge alone** cannot change our behavior if we are *real alcoholics*.

Please consider this: What is in your subconscious mind? None of us have much of a clue, do we? But professionals tell us that stored in the subconscious mind is a memory of everything that we have ever seen, felt, observed, or experienced. The conscious mind cannot recall all that, but it's there. And it influences every idea, emotion and attitude we have. And those ideas and emotions and beliefs—not our conscious minds—determine how we really feel, what we believe, and ultimately what we *do*. If we are to stop being self-destructive and drinking because of things in our subconscious minds that make us restless, irritable, and discontented, we have to get free of all the subconscious things that make us *feel* as we feel and *do* what we do even when it makes no sense. We have to give up our ideas, our emotions and our old beliefs that were programmed into us because they are not resulting in a happy life. Why? One study revealed that 85% of our basic beliefs are learned by age seven. The other 15% of what we come to believe in our lives is filtered through what we learned by age seven; therefore, researchers suggest that most humans have beliefs that have been accepted with a seven-year-old level of consideration. Many in our fellowship have confessed that they are "children in adult bodies" or "an adult body with a teenage mind." That is because of the subconscious beliefs that were put into place when they were children or teens. Few adults ever stop to list all their belief systems and test them against available facts or against newly-learned truths in order to see if they really hold up under the scrutiny of objective review. No wonder, then, that many alcoholics describe themselves as "a child in an adult body" or "a teenager in a full-grown body." Contributing further to the dilemma is the fact that emotional development is arrested when children are traumatized, and new studies suggest that trauma was often a prerequisite for—and contributing factor to—the formation of an addictive personality.

So let's review. We have an illness with a physical aspect and a mental aspect: there are things in the subconscious part of your mind that you don't even know are there but that really make you do what you do, think the way you think, believe the things you believe and feel the way you feel. We *say*, using our conscious minds, that we'll quit drinking, but the subconscious mind has a record of times when we were restless, irritated, discontent, or bored and we drank and it gave us ease and comfort. Later, it quit working when the negative effects became greater than any perceived positive benefit. But that message of "relief" remained in the subconscious brain even as our conscious minds were telling us, "I really have to stop doing this—I'm destroying myself and it's not giving me relief anymore."

So even as we stopped getting all the past results we sought, trying over and over unsuccessfully to recapture a former experience, the subconscious mind kept telling us a lie: that it will be different this time; that we will enjoy it this time; that we can control it this time; that it'll work without negative consequences and will give us relief this time. We believe lies, and most would agree that it is insane to believe lies. Can you admit to your innermost self that you have done things in the past or that you have made some recent decisions that were not in your best interest—things, for example, that are unhealthy to your body, physically? (Answer) Is it sane to do things that are unhealthy to our bodies or that disturb our peace of mind? (Answer) Then we need to be restored to sanity, so let's address that truth.

STEP TWO says: **"Came to believe that a Power greater than ourselves could restore us to sanity."** The insanity referenced in Step Two refers to our belief systems which cause us to believe deceptions which result in unmanageable, miserable lives. On first seeing a step about restoring us to sanity, we hated the thought that someone might accuse us of acting crazy at times—drunk or not drunk—but then the literature tells us, "The first thing apparent was that this world and its people were often quite wrong." That means, all people—not just alcoholics—often aren't quite right! George Bernard Shaw said that the earth is the insane asylum for the universe, but we cannot do anything about the insanity of others. In fact, since we consciously say we're going to do one thing but then *do* the opposite, we obviously can't do anything about our own crazy behavior, either. So we are powerless over both our minds and our bodies. Can you look at some of your past experiences and relate to that? (Answer) Can those of you who have been dry for any period of time see that, even though you have been dry, you have done some things that were self-destructive or harmful to your relations or best interests? (Answer) Can those of you dry for any period of time see that you're currently addicted to something else that is also harmful to you? (Answer) Is it sane or insane to use substances that we know are harmful? (Answer)

Step Two tells us that there is some power that other alcoholics before you—who were just like you—have found that made them stop believing lies such as "maybe *real alcoholics* can drink as normal drinkers some day" or like, "My behavior *used* to be insane but it's not insane any more." That power can restore us to sanity so that we can automatically react sanely and normally to alcohol by not using it and so we can automatically react sanely and normally in life without alcohol. The "automatic" part comes, we are told, by the time we work to Step Ten. The power manifests in the form of sanity within us. More importantly, that power, which the literature calls a "higher plane" thought-life that we are capable of thinking on, can guide us through the day, away from insane behavior to sane, non-self-destructive behavior. Because part of our problem centers in the mind, let's see what a former chief administrator of a Texas mental hospital told one member of our fellowship: *"We lock people up in this institution for two reasons: (1) either they're in delusion so they can't see reality and can't tell true from false, so they can't be honest with themselves; or, (2) they tend to hurt themselves or others or both."*

Can you admit that you have done some things that are harmful to yourself, that were self-destructive? (Answer) Do you think that is sane behavior? (Answer) So can you concede to your innermost self that you have experienced the obsession of the alcoholic mind and that you are, therefore, mentally powerless over alcohol? (Answer) Do you concede that an unmanageable life is an insane way to live and that you evidently need some power that you haven't found so far to stop the physical craving, the mental obsessing, the unmanageable behavior, and the crazy behavior? (Answer) Can you see that we really have more of a thinking problem than a drinking problem? (Answer)

We've admitted doing self-destructive things. Those things were based in the thinking that came from what the literature calls your "lower nature," the thoughts that come from your lower self, your false self, rather than your Higher Self or your "spiritual mind." But there have been times when you walked away from self-destructive things, and that was a result of thoughts that originated in your Higher Self or came from your Higher Power within. Have you experienced both kinds of thoughts: creative thoughts as well as self-destructive thoughts? (Answer) Then the Second Step questions are, "Can you concede to your innermost self that there is some Higher Power within you that is greater than the lower nature thoughts that have been driving you? (Answer) Are you willing to try to tap into that power that saved us from ourselves in order to quit doing crazy things and to come up with a new design for living that will result in a happy, manageable life?" (Answer)

Then you have completed Steps One and Two. Now, in Step Three we're invited to make a decision to turn our will and our lives over to the care of some Power that is greater than what we have so far found in our lifetimes. We are told that we must find a new, positive conception of what the Higher Power really is, and that fact brings us to a new and vital idea. Earlier we discussed two parts of the mind: the conscious and the subconscious parts. Now we're going to discuss a third part, which the literature calls the "Universal Mind" or the "Creative Intelligence." The literature tells us that "as soon as we admitted the possible existence of a

Creative Intelligence...we began to be possessed of a new sense of power and direction."

Your concept of the power does not have to be like anyone else's concept as long as you see it as a power sitting dormant within each of us that needs only to be awakened so that we can tap into its "power and direction." We ask, "Might the path to recovery—to being restored to sanity—involve tapping into what the literature calls the "Spirit of the Universe" within us, tapping into our Right Mind rather than the Wrong Mind? Is it possible the literature is correct when it says that *a Creative Intelligence* can provide *a new sense of power and direction?* That "Creative Intelligence" would be the opposite of our human intelligence that has led to an unmanageable life, because our human intelligence led to self-destructive behavior, not creative behavior. That should make it real easy to answer this question, then: "Are you willing to seek such a power that can make you behave more sanely and in a less self-destructive fashion?) (Answer)

The opposite of self-destructive and insane living is called "spiritual living," because one definition of a spiritual person is "a person who has clear and right and logical thinking." So, we are going to discuss something we call "spiritual living," which is just a sane way of living. By the way, we did not work the steps and turn into fanatical saints. We just work at avoiding self-destructive behaviors today, not because our conscious minds tell us to and not because we are saints. We don't do self-destructive things anymore because the spiritual life we lead is just a sane life! Now that makes it rather easy to work these steps, right?

But before we discuss spiritual—or sane—living, we'd like to clear up a few more misconceptions about what spiritual living is about for those who have a problem with "the God part." First, the literature makes clear that agnostics, defined as "people who doubt the existence of a God," can have a spiritual experience. The literature says, "Many who were in that class are now among our members." It also reports, "Surprisingly enough, we find such convictions no great obstacle to a spiritual experience;" therefore, no matter what anyone's beliefs or concepts or past experiences about

God might include, *everyone* can work these steps and gain the benefit.

So from our discussions so far, we see that we need to recover our mental health so that we can avoid doing the crazy things we did in the past. The literature says that "we, who have recovered from serious drinking, are miracles of mental health." Are there any here who do not think that their mental health can stand improvement? (Answer) Well sane living, or spiritual living, is the place to begin the journey to restoring mental health. Again, spiritual living is not an effort to turn anyone into a saint, but we haven't had the degree of stability in life that we'd like, so we suffered from unmanageability. The literature says that spiritually-minded persons—that is, 'sane people'—"were demonstrating a degree of stability, happiness, and usefulness which we should have sought ourselves."

For millions of years, mankind made it quite fine by living with the internal guidance system given to all humans at birth. This system that tunes us into proper directions is within each at birth and it really makes life simple. We need but exercise the intuitive sixth sense to get sane directions every moment of every day. The body-mind complex arrives with natural, self-preserving drives. In alcoholics, those healthy drives were short circuited by faulty conditioning and wrong programming so that alcoholics, and most people, end up with self-destructive drives. Our minds, therefore, need changing, and the change involves getting free of all the faulty conditioning and the wrong programming. No wonder the literature tells us that we must cast aside ideas, emotions, and attitudes! We must cast aside the way we've been thinking, feeling and believing.

Our real problem is becoming clear. It's not about what we're addicted to. It's about those faulty belief systems that drive our subconscious and conscious minds; thus, to speak of our "spiritual status" is to refer to the status of our minds. It is not about our desire to become perfect and it is not about living a glum life. When mental health is recovered, we start bypassing the subconscious mind and start picking up on what we had failed to tune in to from the Universal Mind. If we don't tap into that guidance, we live the same miserable lives we've lived. Why? Because we are driven by all the things in the subconscious mind that make us do insane, destructive things, and that can happen drunk or not drunk. We must seek guidance from a different part of our minds.

We're told that there are only two groups that do not recover their sanity and their physical health: (1) those who are so stubbornly self-destructive that they refuse to follow the 200 words—the steps—so they never recover full sanity; and (2) those who cannot be honest with themselves. Anyone else can have spiritual experiences and come to a needed spiritual awakening since our spirits have been asleep, unconscious of guidance. So anyone capable of honesty can become sane by getting in touch with what the literature calls the "Universal Mind" or the "Creative Intelligence." Let's talk about that.

Compare a "spiritual malady" to a muscle that has shrunk and grown useless from not being used. Each of us has a Spirit or Universal Mind or Creative Intelligence or higher-thought-system or a Higher Power to guide us sanely through life. But just as an unused muscle weakens completely, so did our internal guidance system. The steps give us a method for tapping into that guidance that we have been ignoring. Ignoring it, not seeking it in the peace and quiet and stillness, left us to use our conscious minds to try to get through life, and our experience proves that doesn't work for anyone. Why? *Because we can't do what the conscious mind says we're going to do.* We've been following the dictates of the subconscious mind even as we consciously tried to stop but couldn't.

Thus we see major insanity, not just among alcoholics, but among our society as a whole. We were given beliefs by society, parents, teachers, preachers, and others…but those were not *our* values or *our* beliefs. And they weren't even *their* beliefs—they were just passing on what they *heard*. We didn't weigh out all possibilities and then *choose* those beliefs. We didn't even get to choose our own names, for gosh sakes. And we were programmed to respond to those people and their demands by a system of reward and punishment, defined in our homes by whatever methods our parents used and defined in the culture by people who want to try to control us and make us follow their beliefs. Now we see again why the literature says that we must cast aside ideas, emotions and beliefs. Hanging onto them results in nil, we're told. Much of our insane behavior comes from our efforts to get rewards or to avoid punishment, still acting like children. That proves to be rather unproductive for adults.

Destructive behaviors occur when we allow self-will to guide us rather than being guided by the Will of the Universal Mind, which some call "The Higher Power" or "The Higher Power Within." Why? Because one Will—our Higher Will, drives us to happiness, joy, and peace, while the other will (self-will or our lower will or ego) drives us to the gates of insanity, to self-destructive behavior, or to death. So, let's talk about wills and ego.

There are some "understood" words in the 3rd Step that we can insert. What it really tells us, when we insert the understood words is (We) Made a decision to turn our (self or lower) will and our (unmanageable) lives over to the care of our Higher Power, or to a thought-life originating from a higher plane, to use a term from the literature. So the real problem is that we have been living a life run on self-will (that is, the *will* to *self*-destruct, the will of the physical mind, or ego, or arrogance) instead of the sane will within (the desire of which is that we be protected, happy, joyous, and free). So how do lives run on the Higher Will of the Creative Intelligence differ from lives run on our self-destructive-will? Here's how:

THE *CREATIVE INTELLIGENCE* SAYS:

1. "Harm no one"
2. "Be humble"
3. "Judge no one"
4. "Do not try to control others"
5. "Love all"
6. "Serve all"
7. "Be still"
8. "You already have everything you need"
9. "I will guide you...just follow my guidance"
10. "I will provide for you"

11. "I will change you"
12. "I know all and you only need my directions"

The *LOWER NATURE,*
EGO-DOMINATED MIND SAYS:

1. "Harm people...lower them to elevate yourself"
2. "Feel important"
3. "Criticize and judge all"
4. "Let me control everyone"
5. "Fear all—assume a defensive posture...or an offensive posture"
6. "Use all"
7. "Go...do...zoom!"
8. "You do not have enough and you never will"
9. "I should be able to guide people—they need to listen to me"
10. "I will provide for myself just the way I always have"
11. "I hate change"
12. "I need to know more, to know everything, and I need it now"

There are only two sources for what inspires us: those inspirations which come from the higher plane or the thoughts which come from the lower nature. Which of those two would you think was driving us when we were acting insanely? (Answer) So self-will and ego and fears and destructive thoughts from our lower nature—from our subconscious minds—are a source of insane behavior. Since our egos and our arrogance form the core of all our problems, let's talk about the ego.

In the fellowship, we talk about "peeling back the layers to find our truth." What are our layers? Imagine a ball at the core surrounded by another outer layer and then a second layer and then a final outer layer. These are the various parts that make us up:

1. The Real SELF—the sane, Spiritual Self—unfortunately hidden at the deepest level—the core.

2. The false self—my self image or images that I try to maintain

even though they're not the Real Me. Those images—the false personas or roles played—are the part of me that drives all emotional intoxication. The personas can form many layers, all of which separate me from knowing my Real SELF.

3. The ego. (In Latin, "ego" means "I"—the false "I.") The real damage comes from the use of ego-defense mechanisms—things like, "denial," "justification," etc.—that are really just the tools that the ego uses to defend the false self, to defend my "image" which is based in the lies I tell and the lies I believe about my "self"—the mental lies I believe about me.

4. The physical body, the outermost layer, which most of us focused on all our lives.

So the ego and the defenses we used to protect all the false images that we created are really just a set of tools that we use to protect and maintain the false self-image or the false images that we show the world. We'll discuss the tools of the ego in Step Six. Because the ego is about protecting something that is a lie, the ego is the liar within us: it tells us lies about ourselves; it tells us lies about others; it tells lies to cover other lies. The ego is also about fear. Why? When we are driven by our egos and working to protect our false self (-image), we know deep inside that we are living a lie, and the thought of being "found out" leaves us in fear. Too, all ego-states demand the things that each state thinks it needs to continue, and all ego-states fear not getting the things they believe they need to exist! We become self-seeking and we become restless, irritable, and discontent and angry when we don't get what we want. The ego will do everything possible to keep us from seeking quietness or serenity. As far as the ego is concerned, life is a battleground and we are to be fighting and struggling every moment. *Every* moment, according to the ego, is reduced to a life-and-death issue. Since all issues become life-and-death issues, we overreact to everything in life when living in ego. We get in an argument with a spouse and shout, "She's killing me!" or "He's killing me!"

The will of our Higher *SELF*, our Real *SELF*, is that we be at peace, meaning having peace of mind. That state of peace can only originate from the higher plane of our internal guidance system because the ego—getting its inspiration from our lower nature—cannot tolerate giving up its delusional fight for life. We are constantly at war all right, but the war has always been internal, even as the ego was telling us that the enemies were "out there." The literature says that we are like "Jekyll and Hyde." That's true, because we have a set of beliefs and many identities or roles that are given to us by this culture that are in direct conflict with the values of our Higher Self. Because our society is a "can't ever get enough" kind of society, that message is in our subconscious minds. No wonder we were never satisfied. No wonder we were in conflict. The Higher *SELF* was telling us that we are complete, that we are enough, but society and its offspring—our ego—were telling us that we are not enough and that we don't have enough and that we never will have enough and that we will be abandoned and alone because of that. That is why we are driven to get more and more—believing society's concepts of the "Principle of Scarcity" and the "Need for Accumulation." Those two dominant concepts send us the message that, since we'll never have enough and will never be enough, we better get more; therefore, the drive for more comes directly from the ego. And the drive for more assures that we will never be satisfied, so dissatisfaction comes from the ego. See why we're in trouble if we want to do things as planned by the conscious mind: our conscious plans are often overridden by the conditioned, subconscious mind. Do you see why we cannot be satisfied and happy unless we tap into the "Creative Intelligence" within? (Answer) See why ego is at the root of our dissatisfaction and our troubles? (Answer)

So let's review: the Universal Mind heals; self-will, being driven by the human, physical mind, kills. The Higher Power's Will is to construct; self-will and ego want to self-destruct. The Higher Power's Will leads to happiness, joy, and freedom; self-will leads to self-destruction and unhappiness. Knowing that, and realizing that the seeking of The Higher Power's Will is spiritual living, and knowing that spiritual living is just sane, non-self-destructive living, it becomes a simple matter now as to which Will we should let guide us through life. In fact, we have no choice. The only choice is to continue with the steps and arrive at a place where we are willing to seek guidance from another source within that we have not been trained to use. To be happy and free, we must learn how to use the tools to tap into that power, that resource within. The alternative is a miserable life which results from being driven by a part of the mind that we are not in control of but that, instead, controls us.

Therefore, in taking Step Three, we are simply admitting to three things: (1) we've tried to manage alone using our human intellect and it's not working; (2) we're turning over the unmanageable part of our life to a new manager, to a Creative Intelligence, to the Universal Mind, realizing that our human intelligence is not getting the job done; and (3) we're making a decision—the decision being to do Steps 4-12 since they are what get us out of self-will and allow The Higher Power Within to manage. So, the Third Step question is this: are you willing to do Steps 4-12 to seek new management that will rid you of ego, that will rid you of insane, destructive behavior and that will rid you of your unmanageable life? (Answer) Then you have done Step Three. We'll confirm our decision by reading APPENDIX ONE in the Workbook in unison. Please turn to the Workbook in the back and find APPENDIX ONE. (All read together in unison. After the reading, the Sponsor/Leader says: "Because you have committed to this course of action, you will never be the same again. Thanks for being here." Now, schedule the next meeting and provide phone numbers.)

*[TO THE SPONSOR OR STEP MEETING LEADER—PLEASE
READ THIS PRIOR TO THE SECOND MEETING]*

To prepare for Step Meeting Two, look over this strategy information. You'll need a copy of the literature in order to have the pro-
tégé(s) turn to the inventory sample columns and read "we were
usually as definite as this example." Make clear that the meaning
of "definite" according to the dictionary is "as limited as" this. The
literature says that this is as detailed as the writing needs to be at
this point. The founders had people give some key words (nouns
or adjectives) that name or describe the faults in people that the
protégé sees. Per the literature, three or four words for each person resented will be sufficient:

Mrs. Jones is a nut, snubbed me, is a gossip.
My employer is unreasonable, unjust, overbearing.
The wife misunderstands, nags, wants the house, isn't as good-
     looking anymore.

You will find that by having the protégés write out four or five
people and give three to four brief adjectives or nouns after each
that you'll really get a clear picture of what the protégé is like.
Remember that the literature says that we want the protégé to see
the *nature* of his/her wrongs at this point, not *every* wrong ever
committed. More will be revealed later through this process. Here
are some typical comments we've been given in inventory:

My boss is a tightwad, demanding, a control freak, is arrogant.
My wife snoops, is judgmental, is unforgiving.
Tom is manipulative, a liar, untrustworthy.
Tanya is a back-stabber, a thief, overly-critical.
My ex-boss was phony, greedy, impatient, expected too much.

STRATEGY

After collecting the data, you'll ask, "OK—whose inventory did you just take?" (Let the protégé see that by following the directions in the literature exactly, he just took their inventory! Then ask:) "Did you notice how strange the example is? I mean, we are supposed to be taking our inventory but the literature guides us to take others' inventory. So what's the deal?

"The deal is what the founders called 'psychological projection.' That is, what we see and criticize in others is what we really hate in ourselves. If you spot it, you got it; if you can see it, you can be it. So now, let's do what we're really supposed to do. Using the truth that 'if you spot it, you've got it,' we can now use their inventory to take your inventory. You see, the beauty of resentments in relationships is that they provide the only tool we have for seeing ourselves. They are our mirror. By the way, what you've written about others might be true. Why? Because the literature says at the end of the inventory example that it is 'apparent that the people of this world are often quite wrong.' But now, this isn't their inventory—it now becomes yours." [Then, you'll take each of those traits the protégé saw in others and find out how that is also a trait of the protégé.] Example: "Let's take the Boss: You said he was a tightwad, but now I want you to tell me when you have been a tightwad." (Answer)

Thus, before the second meeting, you'll need to read the entire Session Two material so you're familiar with the entire process.

STEP MEETING TWO

(TO COVER STEPS FOUR AND FIVE
AND PROVIDE A FOLLOW-UP FOR STEPS SIX, SEVEN,
AND EIGHT)

[Sponsor/Leader Says] You've completed Steps 1, 2, and 3 and we're ready to go to Steps 4 and 5. If a business is failing, it needs new management. That's what we're looking for—new management. We're looking for a new manager to run the business of your life because (a) you admitted that your record shows you need some new management and (b) so that you can relax and take it easy and let the new manager handle business decisions. And the first thing a new manager needs is for you and the manager to take an inventory of assets and liabilities, to see what has been causing the trouble. Remember, we know alcohol was not causing our troubles. What evidence do we have of that fact? Many in the fellowship have stopped drinking alcohol but their lives remain miserable and unmanageable. So we have to identify *all* the traits we have (both positive and negative) and determine what we need to keep and then see what we need to get rid of. In the inventory, we are not looking for all our wrongs. Instead, we are looking for the *nature* of our wrongs, for the shortcomings that are causing us trouble; therefore, you don't have to spend months finding all of your specific shortcomings. We need only see the general nature of your wrongs, the literature says, and then we'll study your assets as well.

Since we all have resentments or have been angry with people, we're going to ask that you turn to APPENDIX TWO in the Workbook in the back and fill in four or five names of people, institutions, or rules you're most angry with and then list three or four things wrong with each. Let me give you an example from the literature of how to fill in the blanks [read]:

Mrs. Jones	a nut	snubbed me	a gossip
My employer	unreasonable	unjust	overbearing
My wife	misunderstands	nags	wants the house

Before we begin, however, please notice that Steps 4 and 5 are about a *moral* inventory while Step 10 is about a *personal* inventory. 4 and 5 are quick and to the point. We cannot recall at this point every wrong we ever did. We are looking for the *nature* of our wrongs, not each of our individual wrongs. So go to the Workbook in back and complete the two columns now.

STRATEGY

[The protégés should only take a few minutes. Allow the writing to begin. Encourage your protégé to move on. Many will want to get too detailed and will try to write the perfect Column One and Column Two. Next, begin to use the strategies read earlier to take the protégé through the inventory process using the following]:
[Ask] OK—whose inventory did you just take? [Let the protégé see that by following the directions in the literature exactly, he just took *their* inventory! Then ask:] "Did you notice how strange the example is? I mean, we're supposed to be taking *our* inventory but the literature guides us to take *other people's* inventory. So what's the deal?

The deal is what the founders called 'psychological projection.' That means, what we see and criticize in others is what we really hate in ourselves. If you spot it, you got it; if you can see it, you can be it. So now, let's do what we're really supposed to do. Using the truth that "if you spot it, you've got it," we can now use *their* inventory to take *your* inventory. You see, the beauty of resentments in relationships is that they provide the only tool we have for seeing ourselves. They are our mirror. By the way, what you've written about others might be true. Why? Because the literature says at the end of the inventory example that it is "apparent that the people of this world are often quite wrong." But now, this isn't their inventory—it now becomes yours. So let's look at the list again:

STRATEGY

[Now what you'll do is take each of those traits the protégé saw in others and find out how that is also a trait of the protégé]

Examples:
Let's take the Boss:
You said he was a tightwad, but now I want you to tell me when you have been a tightwad. (Answer)
You said he was demanding, but now I want you to tell me when you have been demanding. (Answer)
You said he was control freak, but now I want you to tell me when you have been a control freak. (Answer)
You said he was arrogant, but now I want you to tell me when you have been arrogant. (Answer)

Repeat this process for every one of the traits the protégé has listed. The protégé will be shown exactly what her or his liabilities are. With only five people he resents, and with three to four negative traits, you can uncover a dozen or more of the negative traits that reveal the nature of the protégé's liabilities and will show the protégé what needs to be worked on. This method used by the founders was much more effective than asking protégés to list the negative traits that are causing their problems. Here, they experience their negative traits.

[SAY] Now, we can use the list to move into fears. First, alcoholics typically have three sponsoring thoughts: 1. *I am not enough* (that may be "not smart enough," or "not good looking enough," etc.) 2. *I will never have enough* (that can be about money, sex, cars, retirement funds, etc.) 3. Because of 1 and 2, *I will be abandoned.* Why? Some males think, "I have to have money to get her and keep her." Some women in inventory have revealed that they believe, "I need a man to care for me, and I'm not enough so I'll keep him with sex." We can use the list now to show how fears are revealed in the inventory and relate to the three false beliefs many hold about themselves. For example, criticizing the boss for being a tightwad is really about economic fears; that criticism of the boss for being demanding is really about not doing enough at work to keep a job; criticizing the boss for being a control freak is really about supervision fear, fearing that sloppy work might be uncovered if tight supervision is enforced.

STRATEGY

[Do the same with each person listed]
EXAMPLE: Let's look at "the wife":

a. *snoop—Might this really be about the fear that she's going to find out something being hidden and will then abandon? And isn't the fear that, if she abandons, then you won't have enough? Also, inquire into what conduct is inspiring snooping.*
b. *judgmental—Might this be about the fear of being held accountable for your actions?*
c. *unforgiving—Might this involve a fear that, since you've acted like a real jerk, she might not forgive, and then your fear is that you'll be abandoned and she'll get 1/2 of everything and you won't have enough?*
d. *isn't as good-looking—Might this be about a fear of your image being impacted?*

[SAY] Column Three lists the shallow ways that those people or things listed in Column One affect your...

Pride—no one should see me with a woman who doesn't look great—I have an image to uphold
Self-Esteem—I look better; she needs to take care of herself like I do
Ambitions—I want a buff woman to make me feel good about myself
Emotional Security—I am in turmoil around fear and around love
Financial Security—I don't feel like spending my money on a woman

who doesn't look good

Sex Relations—I may not get the quality sex I used to get in the old days

Personal Relations—all of my relations are being adversely affected by my mood

The Third Column question is: "Where have you tried to have a *human* fulfill those seven areas of perceived needs in Column Three when in truth only *The Higher Power* can do that?" (Answer) [SAY] Now, using the same inventory information, we can probe for where your sexual misconduct has negatively impacted your relations:

SEXUAL CONDUCT AND RELATIONSHIPS INVENTORY

STRATEGY

[Tie all of these into the traits revealed in the original inventory as you have the protégé complete each statement]:

[SAY] We'll take some of those traits discussed earlier, such as selfishness, dishonesty, etc. and see what those can reveal about how you've operated in relationships. Please complete these in regards to those you've had relationships with:

a. Here's how I was selfish (Answer)

b. Here's how I was dishonest—maybe you're worried about the boss finding out you've been stealing company goods or company time? (Answer)

c. Here's how I was inconsiderate (Answer)

d. Here's how I aroused jealousy, and before you answer, please remember that there are many ways we do this, and not just sexually. For example, men sitting on the couch while a woman is cooking dinner after a hard day's work will arouse jealousy since most anyone working in the kitchen would feel jealous of that opportunity to come in an relax and be waited on. Now answer. (Answer)

e. Here's how I aroused suspicion—if you don't want to show her affection as before, she may think you have someone else (Answer)

f. Here's how I aroused bitterness (Answer)

Next, using the same inventory information, in column four we are looking at all these cases to find where you were...

1. Selfish? What do you have that you're trying to hang onto? (Answer) What loss are you really fearing? (Answer) Do you fear the loss of a job or loss of the retirement funds if a spouse leaves? (Answer)
2. Self-Seeking? What does someone else have that you are seeking for yourself? (Answer)
3. Dishonest? Are you telling your wife how you really feel? (Answer)
4. Fearful? (Answer)

If being selfish is of the ego—thinking we'll never have enough—and is that is really an insane feeling, then self-seeking is also insane; and our experiences proved over and over that our dishonesty hurt us, so that's insane; and fears are all based in illusion so that's insane to allow the way we feel to be determined by illusions; therefore, the Fourth Column question is: "Where, in each of the cases you listed in Column One, was your behavior insane (selfish, dishonest, etc.)?" (Answer)

STRATEGY

[Here's another interesting piece of information you might find helpful to use in inventory, especially around the third part on sex: a doctor who worked with the founders discussed several categories of mental illnesses. In our experience, two mental illnesses seem to cover what we become because of our mental disorder: 1. **sociopaths** *are defined as "people suffering from a mental disorder that causes them to treat others in an irresponsible, harmful way; people who do things that hurt others, either physically or psy-*

chologically"; "people who cannot tell right from wrong, true from false, and thus cannot function in society." 2. **masochists** *are defined as "people suffering from a mental disorder that causes them either to hurt themselves or to allow others to hurt them— and to tolerate all sorts of harmful things either physically or psychologically—especially if they can attain sexual pleasure in the process." How many of us put up with harmful words and behaviors and other costly things because the person giving us all that grief at least gave us sexual pleasure?*

[Now, SAY] Really, isn't it amazing, considering the way we have lived, that we would think we have the right to criticize *anyone*, especially when we're only seeing in them the very faults that are in us? (Answer) Can you see that you have done some things to people that need forgiving? (Answer) What are the odds that they are going to walk up to you out of the blue and say that they forgive you? (Answer)

Now that you see these defects and the nature of your wrongs, and now that you know that those defects contributed to the wrongs you've done, and since they contributed to your life being unmanageable and insane at times, don't you want to get rid of them? (Answer) Remember, we can call on the Creative Intelligence within and ask that we become aware of what that Power would have us do so we can receive sane guidance in the future and correct the errors of the past. Are you ready and willing to ask for that? (Answer) Then you've completed Steps 4-6. Now, we're trying to have a spiritual awakening, an awakening of the spirit within which we have not been communicating with in the past. So let's address that spirit and awaken it, now. Please turn to APPENDIX THREE and we'll read it together. (Turn to APPENDIX THREE in the Workbook and read that appendix in unison.)

[Now, SAY] Finally, we're told to return home and review everything we've learned. To assist with that, a guide is available in the Workbook that you can use to uncover any other liabilities that we've overlooked. We focused on the "nature" of your wrongs. At home, you'll be asked through the guide to really get specific, to be thorough, as you look at wrongs done and at wrong thinking. Please take whatever time in needed tonight and in the time before the next meeting to complete the APPENDIX FOUR guide in the Workbook in the back and bring it with you to the next meeting. To be thorough, as the literature suggests, APPENDIX FOUR will guide you in detail as you sit alone and look at yourself painstakingly. It will take some time, but it will be worth it to find all the truth, so please list something in every blank provided. Then, when you finish that work and see all your shortcomings that you want removed, turn to APPENDIX THREE once more and read that out loud again in the privacy of your home in relationship to any new shortcomings you've uncovered and want removed. Thanks for being here. See you next meeting. (Please note: Should you feel at some point that you or your protégé needs additional moral inventory, we have included traditional inventory forms in the Workbook. Please see APPENDIX EIGHT.)

STEP MEETING THREE

(To cover Steps Eight and Nine)

[Sponsor/Leader says] Welcome to the third meeting. We took the first six steps to find our truth. At this point, many of us realized for the first time ever the harm that we put out into the universe under the influence of our wrong thinking which led to harmful behaviors. Thus, many of us experienced remorse or guilt. But if you'll turn to APPENDIX FOUR for a moment, let's look at the asset side of the lists of traits there. You'll see what is really inside you that the liabilities blocked off. We'll see what can manifest if you're guided by the higher-plane thoughts. (*Turn to the ASSETS list in APPENDIX FOUR and read aloud the assets that can manifest in the protégé.*) Now, those things really can manifest, and when they do, we feel useful and we become of real help to others. We also came to see that we had done the best we could, considering our degree of spiritual unfitness, otherwise known as our "insanity." We never got up any morning and said, "You know, I think tonight I'll tell my spouse I'll be home at 5 and really show at 11." We never planned to do anything that hurtful. We really planned to only have one drink—or maybe two drinks—at the most. We did not understand the phenomenon of craving and the obsessive mind. We had no choice. Remember: we are not saints. Let us accept our human side and not beat ourselves up any more. We've done enough of that. As long as we judge ourselves too harshly, we'll surely judge others harshly and will, therefore, never have any peace. But we, at this point, still have to admit more truth about ourselves, so we'll know everything that is wrong and know everything that we need to change and know everything that we need in order to forgive ourselves and others.

So it's time to ask yourself this: "Are you willing to admit to your innermost self that you have harmed some people, that you have taken some things that were not yours, and that you know that you have broken some relationships that need mending in order for you to have any humility and for you and them to have any peace?" (Answer) Then it's time now to clear away the wreckage of our past. We do this by making amends and restitution. "Restitution" is defined as "the giving back of something that was taken away." Sometimes we took money; sometimes we took peace of mind. We have taken many things from many people. It's time to stop that behavior and to make amends.

Step 8 says: "Made a list of all persons we had harmed and became willing to make amends to them all." So, please turn to the Workbook section in back and find APPENDIX FIVE. First, let me share a few more thoughts before you begin writing. Step Eight is much more than making a list. We are told that we are going to "go out to our fellows and repair the damage done in the past." First, therefore, we have to be willing to go. We will *go* to those we damaged or harmed, whenever possible. We are told that only when such an approach is absolutely impossible might we then write a letter or make a call instead. Next, we're going to repair the damage. What repairs are necessary? We cannot know what repairs are necessary unless we know what harm we did. In many cases, the harm seems obvious, but the full extent cannot be realized until we "get into that person's shoes."

Do you see that you closed off a part of the heart in some people by your actions? (Answer) Do you realize that, because a part of their hearts are closed off, others in their lives have been deprived of the fullness of those people and of all that those people could have offered to others if you had not closed off a part of their hearts? (Answer) Do you realize that the people you harmed, whose hearts you closed the door on, can seek help in a thousand places for help but that you already have the key to that door? (Answer) And if you have the key, and if you can open the door to the heart that you closed, do you see why it is imperative that you go to each person and offer to open up each heart? (Answer)

There's another consideration here, too. Remember when we did inventory and you listed the liabilities of others and then found that those defects were really in you and that you were projecting them to others? (Answer) Well as we mend relationships, the liabilities in us drop away and that allows the assets to come to the surface. And, just as when our defects dominated us, causing us to see only defects in others, once we experience the assets within us, that is what we will see in others. Then, we won't be miserable around people. We'll begin to see good in them for we are seeing the good in us.

Thirdly, the refusal to forgive others is really a great example of our own self-abuse. When I refuse to forgive another who harmed me, I live out that harm over and over and over again. By forgiving them, I gain some freedom from the effects of the perceived harm they put out. They might have hurt me once, but I am hurting myself every time I force myself to re-experience it by continually resenting them.

That being said, let's go to your Eighth Step list in the Workbook. I'll pause and give you time to complete APPENDIX FIVE. Just list the names at this point. [*Pause. When the protégé has finished, discuss the harm done to each and have the protégé write a note in the blank to the right, identifying the action that will be taken in each case. Then, continue by saying*]:

Finally, you said that you were willing to go to any length to get the advantages that come through working these steps, so here is the Step Eight question: Are you now willing to go on to Step Nine and begin to make the amends that you must make in order to allow your self-will to pass away, to let The Higher Power's Will come to the front, to return to sanity in order to be happy, joyous, and free? (Answer) Good. Now, we can go to the Ninth Step.

Step 9 says: "Made direct amends to such people, whenever possible, except when to do so would injure them or others." The amends process is explained as the authors tell us what to do: "We attempt to sweep away the debris which has accumulated out of our effort to live on self-will and run the show ourselves." That is what the "action" in the right-hand column of your Eighth Step List will do.

Now, why would I want to make all these amends? First because if I'm making a cake with twelve steps in the recipe and I stop with seven, I will never have a cake. Remember: our founders noted that 90% who went back out stopped at Step Three. Of those who make it past there, 90% of those who went back out stopped after Step Eight. (Notice that after Step Three, in order to do the next step one must face another and confess wrongdoing? Notice that after doing Step Eight, in order to do the next step one must face another and confess wrongdoing? Notice how ego, which does not want to face another and confess wrongdoing, will send us back out to the drink and to die?)

So why make these amends? In order to live, and to live sanely and free! There is a price for everything I do in my recovery work, and there is a price for everything I don't do in my recovery work; there is a reward for every action I take, and there is misery waiting for every action I skip. Next, remember that this is no big deal. This is just one person in the universe going to another person in the universe and saying three things: 1. *Here's what I did, and I'm sorry.* 2. *How can I make this right?* 3. *Is there anything else we need to discuss?* Sometimes we don't like to ask number 3, thinking, "Hey—why open up a new can of worms?" The fact is, anything that comes out after that inquiry is already there inside the person, and if you don't allow it to come out by asking the question, it will stay there and manifest in some other way that will be troublesome in the relationship.

Also, how they react is of no consequence. A man said that he was having trouble making his amends. We pointed out that he was really not convinced that "to drink is to die" because if he were, he'd be doing anything possible—going to any length—to set up arrangements to settle the amends he owes. Remember, the only time Dr. Bob went back out and got drunk after starting this work was when he stopped at Step Eight. Once he sobered up after that binge, in one day he made all his amends and arranged for all payments due to others. He never drank again.

Finally, is it possible for *you* to complete *all* of your amends? Ask The Higher Power Within to give you the strength to do what you must. You know in your Right Mind that the only way to go is to have the peace and freedom from guilt that comes by righting relationships. There is no feeling like the one we get when we make our final amends from this list. It's a level of freedom that very few people experience, which is why you'll seldom hear amends-making discussed and which is a contributing factor to why 90-95% fail to stay sober nowadays. So, how much freedom do you want? (Answer) How soon do you want to get it? (Answer) Then let's get started.

After the Ninth Step another set of benefits will come to you. The literature tells us precisely what is going to happen once we commence to clear away the wreckage of our past. They describe these benefits as "promises." These are the things we are promised to receive before we finish even half of our amends: "If we are painstaking—that means, 'willing to take this pain'—about this phase of our development, we will be amazed before we are halfway through. Halfway would be, if you have twenty amends to make, before you make ten of them these things come true for you. We are going to know a new freedom and a new happiness. We will not regret the past nor wish to shut the door on it. We will comprehend the word serenity and we will know peace. No matter how far down the scale we have gone, we will see how our experience can benefit others. That feeling of uselessness and self-pity will disappear. We will lose interest in selfish things and gain interest in our fellows. Self-seeking will slip away. Our whole attitude and outlook upon life will change. Fear of people and of economic insecurity will leave us. We will intuitively know how to handle situations which used to baffle us. We will suddenly realize that The Higher Power Within is doing for us what we could not do for ourselves. Are these extravagant promises? We think not. They are being fulfilled among us—sometime quickly, sometimes slowly. (The variable there is how quickly we get our amends done.) They will always materialize if we work for them."

Please notice that these promises don't say: "Well, now that

you're making amends, you'll start to have a pretty good day."
Instead, what a message of hope! It is almost beyond comprehension that all of these wonderful events will occur if we make amends
to those whom we have harmed. But, they will happen—that's our
experience. This step is going to bring you into a state where you
are at one with your Higher Self and with others. Now, many of us
are impatient people. We want everything done in an instant. Can
we finish all of our amends in one day, or set up the amends to be
made in one day as our co-founder Dr. Bob did? Maybe not, but
let us ask you this: isn't there at least ONE amends you can make
before going to bed tonight? (Answer)

STRATEGY

*[At this point, help your protégé choose one that he can do.
Also, you might want to role-play the amends, showing how it
could go if the amends is accepted and then how it might go if the
amends is rejected. The protégé will be helped by detaching from
outcome.]* [SAY] Will you go make that amends and then call us
and let us know what happened? (Answer) Great. Are there any
questions? (Answer) Fine, then choose the person here whom
you'll call after you make the amends to discuss what happened with
it. Thanks. See you at the next meeting.

STEP MEETING FOUR

(TO COVER STEPS TEN, ELEVEN AND TWELVE)

[Sponsor/Leader says] Welcome back. We'll be discussing Steps Ten, Eleven and Twelve—the three steps which give us further help in connecting with the Right Mind and with our fellows in order to live soberly, to be happy in sobriety, and to live a sane life. So let's start with Step Ten: **Continued to take personal inventory and when we were wrong promptly admitted it.** Notice that two inventories are required in the step work, and they are different. The fourth step inventory was about "moral" issues. This step is about "personal" (that is, "persona") issues. The ego can return. When? When we accept false *personas* (false states-of-being, false selves, false images) as who we are. We look daily to check to see if we have adopted a new persona or re-adopted an old one, for all emotional intoxication comes from ego, and ego must have an ego-state (a *persona* or false identity) in which to reside. In Step Ten, we are looking for false roles that have come up or come back that will allow ego to return, resentment to return, and then drinking or death to come. (As mentioned earlier, should you feel at some point that additional moral inventory is required, we have included traditional inventory forms in the Workbook. Please see APPENDIX EIGHT.)

We see in Step Ten that only guidance from some other internal system can save us from ourselves—that is, from our false selves. We see that we must find our truth daily through inventory. We must discuss daily any problems with others. We must assure that we have made any necessary amends and that we have stayed in contact with our internal guidance system. We must help others. Why else do Step Ten? We were told that we must "...con-

tinue to watch for selfishness, dishonesty, resentment, and fear."
Thus, we *will* experience those for a time. Don't pressure yourself
to be perfect, but turn from them when they come. The founders
shared their experience: that if we will continue the practice daily,
the obsession to drink will disappear. Listing what we call the
"Tenth Step Promises," the founders tell us: "And we have ceased
fighting anything or anyone—even alcohol. For by this time sanity
will have returned. We will seldom be interested in liquor. If
tempted, we recoil from it as from a hot flame. We react sanely
and normally and we find that this has happened automatically.
(What is a sane and normal reaction to something that makes us
sick and ruins the lives of us and those around us? To say, 'No
thanks' to opportunities to drink! *That's* a sane and normal reaction for us. And if we want that 'sane and normal' reaction, it *must*
come automatically. Remember we tried to think through the drink
and failed. We said we'd control it—or stop—but we failed. The
reaction must be automatic, and it cannot be automatic if we're not
on 'automatic pilot.' Like the planes on automatic pilot that let a
directional beam keep them within set boundaries, we seek in the
morning and throughout the day that kind of direction and guidance as well, so we'll stay on the beam.) We will see that our new
attitude toward liquor has been given us without any thought or
effort on our part. It just comes!" So we don't have to "Think,
Think, Think." In fact, our experience has shown it's much better
when we don't. We just sit back and relax now and let our Right
Mind guide us along the river of life. We're like a leaf, floating
along: whether in peaceful waters or turbulent waters, we just float
along. In the end, we see now that it's all the same. Of the three
options to fight, flee, or flow, today we flow. That is the wonder of
it all. Then, "We are not fighting it, neither are we avoiding temp-
tation. We feel as though we have been placed in a position of neutrality—safe and protected. We have not even sworn off. Instead
the problem has been removed. It does not exist for us. We are
neither cocky nor are we afraid. That is our experience. That is
how we react so long as we keep in fit spiritual condition."

How do we keep in fit spiritual (sane) condition? By practicing Steps Ten, Eleven and Twelve daily. What is our reward? A reprieve from the use of booze, from insanity, from fighting. Here are some Tenth Step tools to use throughout the day: (1) Pause. (2) Ask. (3) Turn. Before every action or word spoken, *pause*. Then, *ask*. *Ask* if the upcoming word or action is going to be kind or mean, selfish or giving. *Ask* what the opposite thought might be and if that thought might be better than what you wanted to say at first. *Turn* to that thought if it would be kind. *Turn* from ego-states. *Pause* to become conscious of what the Creative Intelligence might say or do rather than listening to your destructive ego.

There is a reward for having consciousness of the Creative Intelligence, and we attain that consciousness by doing the above procedure. For many of us, our first thought can still be a totally-wrong thought. The second thought, the opposite thought from the first, more often is the real truth. For example: my first, insane thought might be: "I think I'll go in on Monday and tell the boss to shove this job." Our second, opposite thought, which would be less self-destructive, would be: "No, I think instead I'll find another job before I quit this one." Or, my first thought might be, "Hey, my sorry wife left me." The opposite thought might be, "Gee—no she didn't. I ran her off with my conduct." For many of us, the history of our decision-making, in drunkenness or in dryness, has been a timeline of disaster. Thus, we ask The Higher Power Within for guidance and thereby free ourselves (our false selves) from making decisions.

Next, we stay in close contact with others who have a history of doing the work required for them to stay in a sane state of mind. We talk to them so we can tap into that right thinking of theirs and so we can "bounce our ideas" off them for a second opinion. Why? Because some can be deluded into thinking that—since the goal is to become happy, joyous, and free—if our first thought is that such-and-such is going to make us happy, it must be the right thing to do. Some have thought that having an affair with a person already deeply involved in a relationship with another might make us happy. But clearer thinking reminds us of the misery and tension and disappointment of similar actions in the past. And clearer thinking reminds us of the pain involved with being dishonest, being sneaky, having to lie, and ending up in another dead-end relationship. We soon see that the original thought was from the ego, and the clearer thought has to be from the Universal Mind (or the wise input from a sane advisor) because it's going to result in our doing no harm to others and in our behaving honestly, which is required for us to remain sober.

Finally, we test every thought to see if it is from the Universal Mind or from the ego. We ask: "Can this result in something harmful or destructive to me? Will I have to be dishonest to do this? Is it selfish? Am I just seeking something for myself, not really caring about others and the potential harm to them?" If we get a "yes" to any of those, it's ego. We pause. We turn away, even if we think we'll lose some momentary pleasure, for in the long run our experience shows that it will come back to haunt us. We test every thought, word, and action before we let it come forth.

So here is your Tenth Step question: "Will you continue to take daily personal inventory and continue to set right any new mistakes when you become restless, irritable or discontented because self-will has returned"? (Answer) Thank you. Congratulations!

Now, let's discuss the Eleventh Step. Step 11 says: **"Sought through prayer and meditation to improve our conscious contact with God/The Higher Power, praying only for knowledge of God's/The Higher Power's will for us and the power to carry that out."** Our *freedom from insanity* is not a state that will automatically exist from this time forward. Our freedom is the result of daily work which also results in peace (of mind) because we are in the Right Mind for a change. The literature, in discussing Step Eleven, reinforces the fact that we are looking for inner guidance to receive *a new set of thoughts* to guide us. Here are some key words from Step Eleven directions, showing how much it truly focuses on the mind, on thoughts, on the mental:

  *we have to develop this vital *sixth sense*
  *we are seeking to have our *thinking* directed
  *at this point, we can employ our *mental* faculties

*we are seeking inspiration, an intuitive *thought*

*we now have a working part of our *mind*, the Universal Mind, which was not working before—it was dormant

*our *thinking* will be more and more on the plane of inspiration

*as we go through the day, we pause and ask for the right *thought*

Our founders did morning quiet time when they were enjoying a 93% success rate. Our experience is that eventually we found that during our morning quiet time, we began to spend less and less time with prayers that were telling some Power what we think we need or what we *want* and more time in the quiet...listening for the inner guidance to come forth or sitting in contemplation or consideration. *That* is how we have gotten a new vision, as "A Vision for You" promises. Also, it is the new vision that is giving us sane guidance and that is circumventing the negative influences of the subconscious mind that were inspiring our previously insane thoughts and behaviors. Our experience also shows that the sixth sense, the intuitive thought, appears to us in the form of an inspiration, a symbol, or a vision—hence, "A Vision for You."

We suggest that, at the end of your quiet time, you make entries in a journal of the signs or symbols or images that came to you. In the beginning, you'll get a lot of words and thoughts, but you will eventually progress to a higher level. As we do regular guidance writing, the vital sixth sense begins to work for us. We see that trying to live only a life tuned to the five senses always results in fear, and we see that when we tap into the sixth sense or our Universal Mind, the result is a sense of caring for ourselves and for others. The result is a sense of peace.

Why start out now doing this on a daily basis? Please consider: I had a physical awakening this morning based on an experience I had with my alarm clock. I did not reach a state-of-being physically awake today based on an experience I had with my alarm clock yesterday, the day before or several years ago. So it is with spiritual awakenings: I have to have daily experiences with The Higher Power Within in order to stay awake spiritually on a daily basis. We drink only because we are not spiritually fit (sane). Not because we quit going to meetings. Not because we did not think through the drink—we cannot do that. Only because we don't complete the daily work—and any additional work required—to get and stay spiritually fit (sane). So we seek higher-plane-guidance daily to stay spiritually fit (sane). Eventually, it can come automatically and less work is required and natural living just happens.

In addition to morning meditation, we also receive the following advice about spending a few minutes each night in review: "When we retire at night, we constructively review our day. Were we resentful, selfish, dishonest, or afraid?" This is yet another form of an assets-and-liabilities checklist as well as another form of "Quiet Time," "Meditation," and "Guidance."

So, we ask you the Eleventh Step question: "Just as you had a negative daily routine when drinking, are you now willing to commit yourself to a positive daily routine in which you will spend time each morning to seek guidance? (Answer) And are you willing to commit to spending a few minutes each night in evening review?" (Answer)

To help you get started with this vital step, a guide for Step Eleven can be found in the Workbook in APPENDIX SEVEN. Please get up a few minutes early each morning to use it. Our experience is that we're glad we make that sacrifice. You might soon experience what we did: that it is not a sacrifice at all but is actually a perk.

Here's another part of the logic behind doing daily quiet time: we know that our subconscious minds, the storehouse of all of our unique experiences, make us want to separate from all others. We are powerless to make our lives manageable within tapping into the resource within and are quite capable of returning to insane behavior at any moment if we're not spiritually fit. It is spiritual fitness that results in sane thinking and sane behavior. As we were told in the beginning, we have a thinking problem, not a drinking problem. Yet our experience shows that there is a Universal Mind that can lead to the Right Thought in every case that puts us at peace and in harmony—the by-products of sane living. Since our new thinking impacts our behavior in a positive way, Step Eleven is the basis of behaving sanely and normally. We have no choice about whether we do this step or not if we want to maintain sanity and behave in a normal fashion.

Also, many of us also changed our playmates and play places. Absorbing the negative energy of negative people has a negative impact. Rather than try to change others or to accept exposure to negative energy, we are sociable and pleasant but then we dismiss ourselves. That makes our days more pleasant. Now, to the evenings. Before bed, we reserve a few minutes for the review you said you would do. To prepare for that review, some of us relax for five minutes and then we pledge not to drift into worry, remorse, or morbid reflection around the day's activities as we review. Next, we ask the review questions in APPENDIX SIX. All of that might sound difficult, but it gets easier the more we do it, and we're talking about a total of an hour or so per day to work at building peace. How many hours per day did we spend drinking or hung over and fighting? We soon don't want to miss the quiet time or review time.

Next, how do we know if a message is really from the Right Mind or not? Well, the literature told us to cast aside 1. our ideas (that is, all our thoughts) and 2. our emotions (the reactions of my ego-states) and 3. our attitudes (all our beliefs). So we always look for the opposite thought of our first thought to see if it might be more giving, more honest. To replace all of our old ideas, emotions, and beliefs, we receive a different vision from within.

Secondly, we're told we'll get true, pure feelings, originating from the resource within. These pure feelings replace the emotionally-intoxicating reactions inspired from the destructive human intelligence and the ego that goes with it. So here's another instance where we test our thoughts and words and actions to see if we're being guided by our Right Mind or by things in the subconscious that want to destroy us. We ask, "Will the result be true happiness and not just a physical pleasure that often resulted in so much trouble in the past? Will the result be peace and a sense of relief? If the honest answer is "no," then one is being influenced by the ego.

So to review, we ask, "Can it be that the Power is sitting dormant within each of us and only needs to be awakened so that we can tap into its 'power and direction'?" We also ask, "Could a Force that can bring about a mental change be the reasonable part of our mind as opposed to the insane part of the mind that has been guiding us?" Sane, we give up self-destructive behaviors because we are being guided by the part of the mind that is Creative (Intelligence) as opposed to our self-destructive human intellect. We stop hurting ourselves or others. *That's* spiritual living; *that's* sane living.

Now, let's move on to the Twelfth Step. Step 12 says: **"Having had a spiritual awakening as the result of these steps, we tried to carry this message to alcoholics and to practice these principles in all our affairs."** Having made conscious contact with The Higher Power Within, we have something worthwhile to share with others. We see that, to be happy, we must stop judging others and getting angry with their insane behavior now that we have seen our own. But the spiritual awakening is just a part of the Twelfth Step. Let's look at what we have to do to sustain this spiritual transformation and thus sustain our sanity and therefore our sobriety.

We are told: "Practical experience shows that nothing will so much insure immunity from drinking as intensive work with other alcoholics. It works when other activities fail." When we work with others, our lives change. We are told, "This is an experience you must not miss. Frequent contact with newcomers and with each other is the bright spot in our lives." Those who recover help others who need help, but the ultimate goal of the founders was to get people to become independent of human guidance and human intellect and dependent instead on The Creative Intelligence Within. We were just told that working with others is "...an experience you must not miss." You must get to work by helping others through the steps or you will regress into the insanity of drinking or the insanity of suffering from being on a dry drunk. Working with others reminds us of what our conscious minds will forget: that we were really sick mentally and physically and we can be again—very quickly.

Being of service to others is critical to our continued growth and the maintenance of our sobriety. Now all that's left is to practice these principles in all our affairs. What principles? The principles are the truths and solutions that have been revealed through working the steps. So we ask you the Twelfth Step question: "Will you carry this message to other alcoholics and practice the Twelve Step principles in all your affairs?" (Answer)

So that's it. Congratulations! You've completed the steps. Further options to help the physical body and to address the emotional aspects will be offered. Regarding sponsorship and working with others, don't be hesitant to read this guide exactly as is until you become familiar enough to "wing" some parts. Those who have gone through the steps once can now take the guide and find another drunk to sit down with and use the guide to take them through the steps or to sit together and take turns reading alternate pages of the guide and doing the deal together or in groups. Also, for further growth opportunity, we have provided in the Workbook a "Twenty-Day Growth Plan" as an optional set of exercises. Please see APPENDIX NINE.)

CHAPTER 23

"FOR FLOYD, 'MORE HAS BEEN DISCLOSED'"

So what happens if the old thinking or the old behaviors return? What if the pink-cloud early days and rosy-outlook later days wane and the gray clouds return and the rose-tint fades into darkness again? The step work treated a major portion of my problems: the personality disorder and the wrong thinking. Spiritual disciplines can provide a follow-up to try to keep the personality disorders subdued. But what if we have something more than personality disorders? What if we still behave in ways that are beyond our mind's control even after we do all of the step work and spiritual disciplines? What if Bill W. was right and we need help to become mentally sober, physically sober, and emotionally sober? What if there is more that some need after all the step work? What if the literature is right and our *bodies* truly are different? What if some of the things that trouble us are organic, rooted in body organs and chemical imbalances?

Years after working the steps with Mark and enjoying my life in the remaining glow afterwards, I came to realize that something still was not quite right. Like a car with corroded spark plugs that ran a little better after adding a fuel treatment, I was still not "hitting on all cylinders." Mark also saw that the same applied in his case, even after two decades of doing spiritual work "like a mad-dog." Even after all of our spiritual work, we had not paid enough attention to the fact that the founders told us that we have an illness of the mind and the *body* (as well as the spirit and the emotions). Our spiritual work—along with the mental work that we did—left us sane enough and motivated enough to pursue answers about questions that yet remained about how alcoholics can best treat the other parts of our illness that Bill W. identified but that we had ignored. We were fortunate enough to meet some key people who crossed our paths with new answers. They began by treating our physical (*body*) needs first.

Some might relate to my experience after doing the work with Mark. For a time, I became a "spiritual giant." That actually became a new state-of-being, a new false identity. Eventually, along with that identity came the discomfort of incongruity, where the inside stops matching the outside. As I was seen as a spiritual giant by others but knew that was not my truth, I had to increase my spiritual disciplines in order to try to make the inside feeling align with the outside appearance that others thought they were seeing. All of those efforts still did not address the things inside that were still troubling me. I felt that some parts of my life needed a fine tuning that included more than all of the tremendous benefits that I had received through sincere step work and intensive spiritual work.

Interestingly, some people can sail right along if they are in either a positive or a negative state of congruity, whether their combination is (a) chaos on the inside and chaos on the outside or (b) peace on the outside and peace on the inside. It is the lie of trying to show a peaceful outside while no peace exists inside that creates the frustration and self-loathing that comes with living the lie.

Having been restored to enough sanity, I eventually realized that I was not feeling as well as I had thought. I had claimed wrongly that "I feel wonderful" and really thought I did. Like some other alcoholics I've met, I suffered from dissociation of body and mind. I had experienced the abnormal for so long that I really had no clue what normal actually felt like. The best my group could advise was still the same, telling me I didn't have enough faith, was not praying with enough faith, and was not working my spiritual disciplines as rigidly as I should. Those charges were all false—a fact made clear when a team of professionals diagnosed the other parts of my illness and ended what was still troubling me. Before finding that team, something was still lacking in spite of years of great effort and true faith and rigorous practice of spiritual disciplines. The literature told me that more would *be disclosed* as time passed. Such became my experience.

CHAPTER 24

"WHAT CAN WE DO IF WE'VE DONE IT ALL BUT SENSE THAT WE STILL NEED MORE?"

I knew something was missing. I knew that I had done every-thing as told...and more. I knew that the literature endorsed pro-fessional treatment if required, so I began to search earnestly for more help. I went back to the writings to see if I might find clues to guide me, and I began to talk to people in the medical and men-tal health business and to research what else had *been disclosed* recently about the illness of alcoholism. Seeing the advances made in the sciences in the last seventy-five years, I could not ignore the prediction in the literature that told us that more would *be dis-closed.*

My re-reading of the literature took me back to the founders' early focus on the dual nature of the illness and on their later focus on the four-fold aspect of alcoholism. Through my revived efforts, I would learn the significance of the founders' talk about an ill-ness of mind *and* body, and I would be shown how significant a role the *body* organs were playing in affecting my feelings, my thoughts, and my behavior. Many behaviors that I thought were rooted in wrong thinking or a wrong mindset or a lingering spiritual mal-ady were actually influenced by my under-functioning body organs! I had no idea, but learning that showed me that Bill W. was right when he spoke of a four-element illness that required treatment of the body and the mind and the emotions as well as the spirit. What I found after much step work was that I had not gotten total freedom from anxiety, from obsessive thinking, compulsive behaviors, from a lack of energy and focus, from occasional depression, from the effects of P.T.S.D., and from other addictions that were still harmful. I had to ask, "What's the problem?" To find the answer to that question, I returned to the literature and read:

1. *Sometimes there are cases where alcoholism is complicated by other disorders. A good doctor or psychiatrist can tell you whether these complications are serious.*
2. *God has abundantly supplied this world with fine doctors, psychologists and practitioners of various kinds. Do not hesitate to take your health problems to such persons.*
3. *We should never belittle a good doctor or psychiatrist. Their services are often indispensable in treating a newcomer and in following his case afterward.*
4. *The fellowship does not take any particular medical point of view, though we cooperate widely with the men of medicine.*
5. *Upon therapy for the alcoholic himself, we surely have no monopoly.*

I gained the courage by reading those passages to admit that the step work I did with Mark and all the follow-up work I did alone were all vital but that the literature endorsed other avenues for treatment of whatever continued to nag me. The writings made clear that the founders had no problem with members being treated by skilled people outside the fellowship. I learned that their original plan had always called for additional treatment for most *real alcoholics*. The steps worked on my spirit and helped improve my mind. Behaving more sanely, I stopped part of the harmful behaviors to my body, though not all. So improvement of the mind and the body did follow my spiritual work, just as the literature predicts. But not harming myself more in some ways still did *not* heal the parts that *had* been harmed. Since I had an illness of *body* and mind, I determined to investigate the role my body was playing in the way I *felt* and the way I was *behaving.*

My research revealed many interesting facts. For example, I learned that mood is often determined by my diet on any given day. I discovered that there was a physical-chemical cause for my mood changes. I found that foods are generally either "acidic" or "alkaline" and that excessive amounts of alkaline foods for my body type will lead to a swing in my moods toward being "down" or depressed or anxious or restless or irritable or discontent. I learned that mood swings can indicate something about my *body chemistry* and not necessarily about my lack of *spiritual fitness.* I found that depression can often be either organic or situational and that step work can impact the situational but not the organic depression. Where I once believed that supernatural forces could treat both supernatural and natural deficiencies, I came to see the truth of the statement that "God will not do for you what you can do for yourself."

I learned that the natural organs in my body had been adversely impacted by wrong diet and by the breakdown in the food chain in the world today. I found out that when the natural chemicals in my body are out of balance, it will impact the way I feel and think and behave—no matter how much I try to tap into that Creative Intelligence. I really believed that the power of prayer would suspend the natural laws of nature for me and automatically reverse the negative effects of years of wrong diet and inattention to proper care of my physical body. That thought proved not only to be naïve and arrogant but also almost deadly.

My lazy side did not like what I realized. I found that taking the actions required to treat the deficiencies in my body happened to fall into the category of "What I Must Do for Myself." I also noted that it is something I did only after having been restored to sanity via step work, but not before. Mark urged me for years to begin an exercise program, but I learned in my case that when *organic* depression remains after all the step work and spiritual disciplines have been done, then we can remain immobilized and lethargic. Even knowing that his advice was right, I was unable to engage in that part of the body-healing, body-improvement process. I made some efforts from time to time, but I was never able to stick to a regimen. In spite of the faith I had in his advice because of the positive effects I had experienced, I still remained unable to follow that counsel when he offered it. I reviewed Bill W.'s comments about four types of sobriety: spiritual sobriety, mental sobriety, physical sobriety, and emotional sobriety. I became convinced that I really did need more treatment to address the other areas of healing that he discussed. I needed further mental healing, further physical healing, and further emotional healing. I began by focusing on the physical healing with as much vigor as I had applied in working on the spiritual malady.

*

PART THREE

THE PHYSICAL

*

"SINCE THE FOUNDERS SAID I HAD AN ILLNESS OF BODY AND MIND, WHY DID I NOT CONSIDER WORKING AS HARD ON CORRECTING THE BODY AS I DID THE MIND?"

While we divided our book into parts to share our experiences in seeking the four levels of healing and sobriety discussed by Bill W., we found that no real divisions exist. All in this manifestation, we discovered in our case, is but one whole. That required for us a holistic treatment approach to bring about healing and to give us all four levels of sobriety.—Mark and Floyd

Mark guided me through the steps and I made my amends to others. I definitely had a spiritual experience and a spiritual awakening. However, I overlooked one of the most important amends that seems to be left off too many amends list: *I failed for many years to make an amends to myself.* I failed myself completely by not making an amends to my *body.* The spiritual work succeeded in removing the situational depression of my spirit. I reveled in that glow for a time, yet I would not know for years that organic depression still plagued me. Under the influence of the organic depression, which the step work did not address in my case, I could not exercise. Nor did I take proper nutritional care of my body. I continued to take what I thought was an easier and softer way by ignoring my body needs and by not making amends to it. I did not know that three different body types exist, and I did not seek out a proper food plan for my particular body type.

I ultimately found that trying to use a supernatural treatment to address the under-functioning, natural body-organ components of my illness left me in a very poor state in the long run. I saw a news report of a couple being tried in Colorado for allowing their daughter to die by refusing to let doctors give her the medical care she needed because the parents choose to rely on prayer alone. I realized that I had been taking the very same approach with my own body. I saw that some psychic change occurred via the spiritual exercises that Mark and I did together that affected my Addictive Personality Disorder, but my experience proved that my *body* and mind had other problems that all the spiritual work in the world obviously did not address. I returned to the literature again and read where it suggests using other means outside the fellowship for addressing those parts, recommending "psychologists and psychiatrists and other practitioners." Fortunately, the step work I did with Mark left me sane enough to know that something was still not right, that something yet needed to be done. My search continued.

I was fortunate enough to find a team that was truly effective in treating (a) the other physical liabilities that were ailing me and (b) the other mental and emotional liabilities that were holding me back. They were capable of doing so in my case without suggesting that I use psychotropic drugs. I saw again that the step-work-portion of the treatment only took the founders a matter of hours and that the subsequent efforts involved with bringing about full recovery came in the months or years following as members were guided to those who could address all the needs of the *body* and all the needs of the mind in order to heal. I reviewed the wonderful results of doing the steps with Mark: that work certainly prevented any further damaging of my body with alcohol. But I was still using other things. I was still putting other things in my body that were harmful, such as wrong foods, excessive caffeine, excessive food, *ad infinitum*. I saw how prevalent substituting other addictions after giving up alcohol was with me and how those new practices can create new physical damage. I learned how certain organs in my body impact the way my mind works. As the writings promised, more was *being disclosed.*

With Mark's guidance, I traveled all the avenues suggested in the literature, but in my case there were additional steps I needed to take. "The Other Steps" lifted me over the last three walls that stood between me and total independence, total happiness, total joy, and total freedom. Why had I hesitated for too long to seek the additional help I needed? Because I had been told, "You've reached the end of the road. We are the last stop. Either you get it from us or you don't get it. All you need is more faith and more prayer and that will heal everything." I allowed such comments that contradicted the writings to delay seeking the professional help that I needed.

I little realized that my body organs were screaming for treatment and truly needed healing. My spirit had been treated, and my spiritual state was much improved, yet the other parts—the parts that the founders called an illness of *body* and mind—I ignored. As far as the body-part of the illness, I only focused on the phenomenon of craving and ignored the fact that the founders did much work to treat the *body* and the mind after doing the step work.

Seeing that the founders used outside experts to treat naturally the parts that needed natural treatment, I found the wherewithal to seek more help for myself. Some thought that a sacrilege. Some labeled me a heretic for seeking help from anyone other than them. I almost died around their belief system that *discouraged* me from seeking professional help, but eventually I defended nothing and sought more help. I had seen the truth again in the pages of the writings that *encouraged* me to take advantage of all opportunities to improve. I also saw that, during the days when I parroted the belief that I was in the *one and only* place that had *all* the answers for certain people, I was speaking from a state of arrogance and ego.

I finally had to admit, when I looked at myself and my behavior, that I had become convinced for a period of time that I have "found it," that I have finally "got it." Later, I had enough light fall onto my false reality to make me finally admit something to myself. I said, *Wait a minute! I've been in the fellowship for a dozen years*

but I still have behaviors that are typical of my old addictive per-
sonality when it was at its worst. I think I've made 'progress'
because I've not taken a drink, but I still haven't been restored to
sanity because now I'm overeating, I'm compulsively spending
money, I'm practicing workaholism, and I'm even addicted to the
fellowship. I saw too, in my most honest moments, that I was still
addicted to chaos and was still going after the adrenaline rush.
When I expressed concern about my new addictions, I was told,
"Hey, Floyd, this is about *alcohol,* so stop bringing up anything
else." But enough sanity had been restored for me to know that I
had deeper problems than alcohol and that the absence of alcohol
in my system was not solving my problems.

I had to honestly wonder about my restoration to sanity since
I was still behaving in ways that were self-destructive or that disturbed my peace of mind through faulty eating habits, insane spending habits, etc. Then, I learned that internal organs and chemicals
imbalances can affect my thinking—the thinking that was a core
part of my continuing problem. I had addressed the faulty conditioning that affected my thinking, but I had not known that other
body organs besides the brain have a major impact on my *think-*
ing.

Fortunately, reading the literature again gave me the courage
to seek more when I knew deep inside that I needed more. I did my
spiritual work and was totally grateful for the wonderful results.
Then, I received the black and white test results of a diagnostic
team that analyzed the performance of my organs and also diagnosed my mental and emotional conditions. I was shocked. In spite
of all my prior efforts—completed with tremendous vigor and
prayer and faith and sincerity—I still suffered from *organically-*
inspired obsessive-compulsive behaviors and *organically-inspired*
depression and the lingering effects of post-traumatic-stress-disorder, all of which are alluded to in the literature. What freedom
I was about to gain when I was shown that my continuing problems were not a result of a spiritual malady but were purely and simply...organic! My spiritual exercises *had* worked, and my additional
problems were not from doing the spiritual work poorly or from

still having a spiritual sickness. No wonder all of my increased efforts in that area did not move me over the final hurdles I faced.

I had to be willing to shift beyond the distortion of congratulating myself with thoughts such as *I'm so much better off* and *I'm making progress* to admit that I was still dependent, still not totally sane, and still not free of excesses and of self-destructive behaviors even though alcohol had not been in my body for more than a decade. I believed for a time that I really had the whole deal but saw in my most honest moments that I was yet missing some major pieces. Those pieces were finally identified by a three-part team made up of the very three groups named in the literature! Imagine that. More had finally *been disclosed* to me, and the founders were proved right again.

I came to see that I had settled for partial recovery. I had to consider that more really could *be disclosed* and thus became willing to consider that maybe modern research is right when it shows that the body-part of this "body-mind illness" can prevent me from ever being free of anxiety or depression or compulsive behavior or shifting back and forth in my thinking and behavior. I was not done.

I had to face the truth in my case: there were some things in my body that affect behavior and thinking and feeling and that need correcting. My research also made clear the connection between conditions described in the literature and certain physical and organic aspects that led to some of those conditions. Only by undergoing a full metabolic and mental health analysis did I find a regimen that took me beyond a state of partial recovery to a state of complete healing and peace.

I could not argue that people can be driven by a "hundred forms of fear," but what *was disclosed* was that the hypothalamus is a seat of fear if it is not functioning properly. I learned that an internal *body organ* could trick my mind into believing that false threats or imagined fears are real. I learned that if that organ is under-functioning, I cannot "differentiate true from false." Wow! What a disclosure. I learned that low thyroid function can contribute to a sensation of being "emotionally labile" or emotionally overwhelmed. I learned that a *physical* deficiency contributed to my organic depression, to my continuing anxiety, and to occasions of emotional intoxication. Those states that the literature describes as some of my key problem areas were not rooted singularly in my spiritual malady but were rooted in the deficiencies in my *physical* body.

Is all that just theory? It was until those organs were treated; then, within a matter of weeks I began to *experience* a degree of freedom from obsessing, from anxiety, and from a lack of energy and focus that I had never known before. I experienced the proof that all that was not just theory.

Having found that malfunctions in the body can affect the mind and thus affect behavior, I returned to the writings again for confirmation. Additional reading in our literature convinced me that the body really is a major part of the problem when I read the statements about:

1. a "seemingly hopeless state of mind and *body*"
2. "the *body* of the alcoholic is quite as abnormal as his mind"
3. "we are sure that our *bodies* were sickened as well"
4. "we have recovered from a hopeless condition of mind and *body*"
5. non-alcoholics have been able to stop or moderate because "their brains and *bodies* have not been damaged as ours were"
6. "in working with others, talk about the conditions of *body* and mind"
7. "now about health: a *body* badly burned by alcohol does not recover overnight."
8. there are "fine doctors, psychologists, and practitioners of various kinds. Do not hesitate to take your health problems to such persons" so you can "enjoy sound minds and *bodies*."

My final and ultimate and total healing of mind *and* body came when I again followed the directions in the writings. A re-reading of the literature gave me the "permission," if you will, to seek beyond. It gave me the inspiration to break free from those who were telling me that they alone had the entire solution. I followed the directions in the writings and sought assistance from some "fine doctors and psychologists and practitioners of various kinds." Specifically, I found a cutting-edge *psychologist* who treated alcoholism holistically—addressing the needs of the spirit and the mind and the body and the emotions. She worked with a *fine doctor* who practiced both traditional medicine and natural treatments as well, and the two of them worked with another *practitioner of a various kind*—one who diagnoses the needs of certain internal organs that affect thinking and thus behavior by using state-of-the-art diagnostic methods. I took that additional action as laid out by *some fine doctors and psychologists and practitioners of various kinds*, just as the literature directed, and the result was an entirely new level of healing, of joy, of happiness, and of freedom. Talk and theory transformed into actual, measurable *experience*, and that transformed me into a closer relationship with my True *SELF*.

With their assistance, more *was disclosed*, just as the literature promised. They helped me see that my alcoholism is an illness in which we can experience great pain and suffering because of an addictive personality disorder (APD). They also showed me, however, that the APD was working *in combination with* one or more of the following alluded to in the writings: untreated depression; untreated manic-depression/bi-polar; untreated obsessive-compulsive disorder; untreated post-traumatic-stress-disorder; untreated grave emotional and mental disorders; and/or other serious disorders and chemical imbalances which need treatment. And they showed me how to treat all of those areas *naturally*.

I began following a holistic approach that included therapy for my PTSD as well as nutritional supplements prescribed by a naturopathic physician. I practiced diet modification and I began exercising and have stayed with that regimen. When I began to share how much better I felt, I learned quickly that if people are not up on something, they will be down on it. I can only cite today my experience with the major changes that came after I sought professional help as endorsed by the literature itself. I came to see that body and mind do not function separately. My *experience* was that whatever affects one affects both.

Further research showed me a correlation between what the literature explained and what my doctor revealed. I learned that an under-active thyroid can cause weight gain, mood swings, and fatigue; that under-active adrenals can cause low motivation, lethargy, low energy, and the loss of a sense of serenity. I learned that an acid/alkalinity imbalance can leave one restless, irritable, depressed, and discontent. I found that if the chemicals in my body are out of balance, then I will obsess on things or people and then act impulsively to try to bring my obsession into being; or I can flip-flop between extremes of happiness and misery; or I can suffer depression; or I can constantly alternate between spiritual and material living, between constructive and self-destructive behaviors. And all of that which lingered after years of spiritual work came from my body illness, not my spiritual illness.

I found that my vegetarian diet was suited to only one in three people who are actually of the vegetarian metabolic type; therefore, I *experienced* that no *one* food plan can provide for the needs of *three* different body types. I *experienced* that if one is a protein-vegetarian type but eats vegetables only, he will crash the nervous system and the adrenal system and other organs. That was my experience. As a caution, this should NOT be taken as advice to anyone about what they should do. I would NEVER recommend that anyone abandon cold-turkey any medical program they are on; nor would I recommend that anyone attempt to create their own prescription or non-prescription plan. Those were not any part of my experience.

Mark and I make clear that we adhere today to a plan formulated and prescribed and monitored by a licensed specialist who diagnosed us and created a treatment plan unique for our body types. Each body is different and requires a unique treatment plan. We would never follow a plan that was not implemented and supervised by a licensed professional. Secondly, my caution came from a tragic experience that I witnessed my first six months in the fellowship.

In my original home group, a man was advised in a meeting to get off his medications, assured that God and the fellowship alone would heal him. His sister came into a noon meeting three weeks later, tossed a bag with his anti-depressants on the table, and said, "You people can have these now. My brother killed himself after coming off his medications as the people at this noon meeting advised." I was there and heard others offer him that advice. I was there twenty-one days later when the results of that advice came in. I have never forgotten the truth revealed in that event, so I will risk being labeled a heretic by people who charge that I am wrong to question non-professionals who claim to have *all* the answers to this complex illness called "alcoholism."

Furthermore, I make no claims for anyone else. Does any of the professional help I gained from professionals discount the value of the vital spiritual work that I required and that Mark guided me through? Absolutely not. It reinforces how critically important the spiritual work was and is. I would not have been alive to pursue the other channels recommended in the literature without the spiritual work. I would not have been sane enough to want to seek more help without the spiritual work. But my experience also documents the wisdom of those among the founders who told us that there are four areas which need treatment.

I am asked, "But are we not told that if we address the spiritual part that the mental and physical parts will be healed?" Yes, and my experience supports that truth. Mental and physical healing did come after the spiritual step work. That work shifted me into a non-self-destructive state. In that state, I was sane enough to know when something was missing and then sane enough and energetic enough to do what the literature suggested and seek out those "*fine doctors, psychologists and practitioners of various kinds.*" How significant was the shift, once I began the plan as outlined by the teams of professionals who helped me? It was after a few days on the new plan that I told Mark, "I may know for the first time in my life what 'normal' really feels like."

I also learned that the body and mind either function in harmony with each other or they do not. If they are not in total harmony, they can be brought into harmony by addressing the deficiencies being described in these writings. At least such is what

I found through my own experience. What great joy to learn that the rest of my problems could be treated naturally. What great joy to experience the results. And what great joy to be able to offer an additional course of action to those who come to me and say, "I've done it all, for seven years, ten year, twenty years, thirty years, but I feel terrible" or "I'm worked my rear off with the disciplines but I still feel that something is missing." I can now share what Bill W. pointed out and invite my fellows to seek treatment plans for the other areas that need healing.

Therefore, my experience was that until I addressed the physical aspects of my alcoholism, I did not reach the highest state of peace and serenity and energy. And even after all that, additional help was required for me to reach the fourth level. I revisited the fact that Bill W. also spoke of "emotional sobriety." Mark and I, even after all our spiritual work, our mental work, and our physical work, came to see that we still had additional work remaining for us to avoid the suffering of emotional intoxication and to fixate in a state of emotional sobriety.

*

PART FOUR

THE EMOTIONAL

*

CHAPTER 26

While we divided our book into parts to share our experiences in seeking the four levels of healing and sobriety discussed by Bill W., we found that no real divisions exist. All in this manifestation, we discovered in our case, is but one whole. That required for us a holistic treatment approach to bring about healing and to give us all four levels of sobriety.—Mark and Floyd

By adhering to the plan set forth by *some fine doctors and psychologists and practitioners of various kinds,* the "emotional sobriety" that Bill W. spoke of truly began to manifest at a level for Mark and for me that neither of us had experienced before. The literature speaks of *feelings* returning while also advising us to cast aside ideas, *emotions,* and attitudes. Suddenly that really began to happen for the first time. Clarity came as we experienced the difference in "feelings" and "emotions." We saw how we can merely witness all the feelings that can come and go while at the same time eliminating the emotions that result from ego-states or false identities. The further we became conscious of the Real *SELF,* the more feelings we enjoyed and the more emotional intoxication we escaped. As Mark put it, "That team of *some fine doctors and psychologists and practitioners of various kinds* finally connected the dots and provided the missing pieces of the puzzle."

Some worried that "if we cast aside emotions as the literature advises, we'll become robots." To share my understanding of why the literature would speak highly of *feelings* but negatively of *emotions,* I'll quote a passage from another book I wrote that addresses the difference in feelings and emotions as I experienced them:

Emotions are experienced only by ego-states, by the false selves, and always result in a reaction to something which triggers another reaction to that reaction, and then a reaction to that reaction. The final result is emotional intoxication and insane behavior. Abandoning the false selves causes the loss of nothing except delusion, insanity, and emotional intoxication. Firmly fixed in the True Identity, one lives AS IF and experiences the gamut of true feelings. I might feel anger or I might feel joy. Yet, I am the witness. I see the anger rise; I see the anger subside; I feel the joy when it comes; I see the joy as it goes. But I do not react; therefore, I avoid a chain reaction of events that would leave me intoxicated or insane if I were living in an ego-state and being jerked about by emotional reactions. I do not become trapped in a state of emotional intoxication, for that debilitates and paralyzes. I see so many who are not feeling what they feel over the loss of someone they love but who are experiencing the emotions of an ego-state identity around that perceived loss. They are paralyzed, crippled, basically, dead. At best, they are 'Night-of-the-Living-Dead' creatures. (from **The Twice-Stolen Necklace Murders, pp. 259**)

Much of what Mark and I suffered in spite of all our years of efforts was rooted in emotional influences which we had not cast aside despite the literature's suggestion that we do just that. While physical intoxication was a vestige of a far-away past, emotional intoxication manifested far too often for us to feel completely comfortable. *Why haven't we been able to cast those aside?* we wondered.

We would eventually learn of the powerful connection between emotional intoxication and unresolved trauma. We were fortunate enough to meet a team that works with those alcoholics who have done the steps faithfully and who have practiced their disciplines faithfully but still suffer because of the effects of untreated trauma. Here's what we learned in the process of receiving the treatment that allowed us to move toward what Bill W. called the "Fourth Level of Sobriety."

"TRAUMA AND ADDICTION"

Mark's words still resonate strongly through my being: *At one time I had a belief system that the steps alone would be enough; that belief system almost killed me. I do not pretend to have answers for any other person, but my own experience motivates me to encourage people to look at their own experience.*" Some may look at the cover to this book and admit, "I've moved from the shadowy area of darkness and all the way to the right and into the light." Congratulations. Others may sense that their work has moved them somewhat out of the darkness but not completely into the light. Good progress. Some may recognize that they've really only shifted slightly toward the light. We have hope for those. Some, like Mark and me, may even admit that after years of work and effort, they are still spending too much time in the shadowy boxes. For those, we can share what worked for us, hoping that it might work for you, too. Those who sense that they haven't fixed themselves firmly in that fourth box of light may ask as Mark and I did if more is required to stabilize into that state of lightness—of true happiness, joy, and freedom.

We can ask, "If those with *grave emotional and mental disorders* need more than step work to address the behaviors still manifesting as a result of untreated trauma, what do the *grave emotional and mental disorders* referred to in the literature look like?" For me, they looked like untreated alcoholism, and *that* fact prevented my getting a complete and accurate diagnosis for years. Rather than receiving the specialized treatment for trauma that I needed, I worked even harder to try to make my "addiction treatment" cure my trauma illness. I became more and more frustrated when no results came. I had a square hole deep inside me that I was trying to fill with a round peg.

The professionals who helped us identified twenty typical behaviors of people suffering from untreated trauma. The list is not complete, but between the two of us, we related to all of these. The behaviors that continued to plague us look exactly like what some dismiss as behaviors resulting from "untreated alcoholism," but these behaviors proved to be the result of "untreated trauma."

And the treatment for "untreated trauma" differs significantly from the treatment for "untreated alcoholism." No wonder relief didn't come! Yet we blame no one since the misdiagnosis is easily made. We understand just how easily that error can happen after the professionals specializing in trauma treatment educated us regarding the now-known link between the trauma and addiction.

The understanding we gained regarding the link between the two—and how the trauma was driving our continued suffering— might help others. We only reached new levels of freedom and peace after learning that treatments designed to treat addictions do not erase the unhealthy emotions and behaviors that result from untreated trauma; thus, we needed more. Learning the difference inspired us to seek specialized treatment for a specialized problem, and finding the treatment certainly proved beneficial to both Mark and me. How do we know that our continuing suffering was from untreated trauma and not untreated alcoholism? Because the treatment for alcoholism did not address our remaining problems but the treatment for trauma did. Mark has allowed me to share what we learned when we finally received treatment for our unresolved trauma. The professionals who treated us identified twenty behaviors (1) that were manifesting in our adult lives but were rooted in childhood trauma, (2) that contributed to emotional intoxication, and (3) that had not been addressed by any of our previous work and efforts.

CHILDHOOD TRAUMA

The link between trauma and addiction has now been established by thorough research, so more has truly *been disclosed* about the condition called "alcoholism." Reviewing thousands of inventories and our own experience as well, we found that childhood trauma or adult trauma regularly preceded the use of addictive substances. That being the case, trauma deserves serious attention from us and from many among the *real alcoholics* we work with today. We would feel negligent, therefore, not to share what we have experienced personally. *Real alcoholics* might relate to some of the following information and find that step work alone has not yet addressed all of the components of what some professionals are calling "the number one contributor that sets us up to abuse substances: unresolved trauma."

First, our own inventories and those we listened to revealed that abuse had come to us—and to many we met in our fellowship—in varied forms, including physical abuse, mental abuse, emotional abuse, religious abuse, sexual abuse and/or abuse via outright neglect. Those who can relate to several of the behaviors listed below might find evidence of the lingering effects of past abuse. If any of our readers relate to these behaviors, then you may be like Mark and me: you might benefit from professional treatment for the effects of unresolved trauma.

a. **"Splitting"**—Abused people can become schizoid or can live in duality since the abusers forced on us a desire to be able to control others. How? We wanted to make them stop, so we wanted control. The abused, therefore, often develop a desire for power, internal or external, to use to help make their abusers stop. Also, abused children or adults often want the power to simply be able to tolerate the on-going abuse or to be able to tolerate the continued abuse we anticipate. Others want intervention from some external power that will rescue them or make their abusers stop. We seek rescuers and rescuing. Commonly, the abused child will begin to try to escape.

b. **"Escaping"**—In the dual world that abused people retreat to or that we mentally escape to, *we* are in charge. The groundwork is set for teens or adults to accept offers from others to use intoxicants to try to escape. The abused can imagine their abusers dying; they can imagine telling them off verbally, really exploding on them; the abused can imagine having the power to make them stop; the abused will imagine a "power of good that could intervene in their behalf"—so children love Batman concepts, Superman concepts, Superwoman concepts, etc. The "Deus ex machina" concept has been used in literature for thousands of years and the abused dream about some external power coming to their rescue. We can fixate in a state of immobility, refusing to take action to protect ourselves while waiting for a rescuer to appear or to answer our calls or demands for assistance. We suffer from feeling powerless and helpless and hopeless.

c. **"Repressing"**—When the abused fight back, the abusers usually intensify their abuse. Eventually, the abused begin to repress. We repress our feelings, our anger, etc. Repressed rage boils inside and eventually explodes. The explosions of anger, when they come, can continue into adulthood without the adult knowing the true root of the rage since it rests at so deep a level.

d. **"Desiring Power/Power Grabbing"**—We *dream* about having superpower and we long for some superpower to show up to save us. We want that power in order to have strength and control—control over others to make them stop what they are doing or to make them behave differently. The stage is set early on for us to have a self-will that can run riot as we seek power and try to exert control. So deprived of choice and control early on, we can eventually try to control everything and everyone around us as adults.

e. **"Covering"**—Like the Stockholm Syndrome (where people tend to idealize their captors) the abused often cover for their abusers (partly out of fear or reprisal, partly out of shame, and partly because of "Normalizing" and "Denial")

f. **"Normalizing"** and **"Denying"**—What child or adult wants to be from a weird family? Children will fight on the schoolyard if someone makes fun of a parent. The abused children in dysfunctional families have no models for contrast, so their life is assumed to be the norm. Like a child raised with an elephant in the kitchen, that child believes three things: 1. all families have elephants in their kitchen, and if they don't, they're not normal; 2. believing it's normal to have an elephant in the kitchen, I'll fight anyone who says that having an elephant in the kitchen is not normal; 3. I'll hang with people who had elephants in their kitchen someday and I'll marry someone who was raised with an elephant in the kitchen and we'll have our own kitchen with our own elephant someday. [Our next book on healing relationships plagued by trauma, entitled **Give Me Your Hand—Feel My Scars**, will consider this subject in greater detail.] The abused convince themselves that their parents had to be OK (or "they did the best they could"), because any child and any adult can be driven by ego to think that *we are 1/2 mom and 1/2 dad and if one is rotten I'm 1/2 rotten and if both are worthless, I'm totally worthless.* Because our emotional development is arrested at the age of the greatest trauma, we can delude ourselves and act as if everything is OK. Many abused take those warped perceptions of reality into adulthood. We can mentally convince ourselves that we are fine or that we have now become fine through all our efforts to improve. We can convince ourselves that we are now OK as a result of our work when, in fact, that work only began to tap into the deepest pain. In order to bring about release, we had to be guided to probe more deeply, to get more help. Some of us reached the "spiritual-giant" ego-state and talked about forgiving abusers before ever really have done the work to free ourselves of the effects of their abuse; or we can talk about the abusers as if everything was just fine, really. That allows the trauma effects to remain imbedded at the cellular level and it continues to make us miserable. We sometimes paint a picture of a normal, happy family—the one we wanted but that really never existed. Picturing an abnormal family life as having been normal can become a firmly held belief in an adult's mind. The lie can become perceived as the truth and we do not differentiate the true from the false.

g. **"Avoiding"**—Associated with "Denying" is the use of "Avoidance" techniques by those suffering from unresolved trauma. In order to avoid facing or confronting any of the true sources of our pain, we would shut down or react in anger when anyone tried to discuss the roots of our trauma. We would become defensive or retreat mentally, a practice associated with "Escapism." While we used those mental techniques to escape, we used alcohol to help escape by changing the way we felt physically, mentally, and emotionally. Inside an adult body, we can suffer from a child running like the wind from its past reality that is manifesting in the present.

h. **"Deluding"**—As adults, the abused can continue delusional thinking, imagining that many have loved us and have cared for us. We seek love endlessly and imagine that we've had it, that dozens or hundreds or thousands love us and thank us, therefore evidencing the fact that we are loveable. We seek that approval, that message that we are loveable, since the opposite message was given to us by the actions of certain abusive adults who had power or influence over us. We seek externally to have our Maslow-defined needs met, seeking love, esteem, and fulfillment from others, trying to appear to be good, to be accepted by others, to be accepted by God, etc. Most never recover enough to have the Self-Love, Self-Esteem, and Self-Fulfillment which could make them truly free. If they could reach that state, they would never have to seek power or love from any other person and would never have to create fictional sources of power or delusionally create images of normalcy. Many abused children end up speaking well of abusive parents, repress the abuse beyond conscious memory, lie about the abuse or the abusers, and speak kindly of all those who have loved them or of the most recent sources of power or love that they have found. Concepts are stacked on top of concepts, all to meet perceived, subconscious needs that are purely fictional needs to begin with but that are based in the very real effects of trauma.

ADULTHOOD TRAUMA

i. **"Repetition Compulsion" or "Re-Enacting"**—Effects of past trauma can inspire in adults the Repetition Compulsion. If we have a parent who abused us, we often find a lover who will abuse us. We re-enact that which was familiar. The abused child *thinks* that she/he is "comfortable" with the familiar. The familiar way of life often included being abused, living with chaos, living with unpredictability of those who acted lovingly one minute but as if they could kill us in their fit of anger or rage the next minute. The abused child can become the abused adult, inspiring us to link up with abuser types. The abused also often become abusers themselves. The stage is then set for tremendous fighting when relationships have two abusers together. To get free of the abused child within can help prevent the repetition and the re-creation of toxic relationships and harmful environments.

j. **"Parent-Child Role-Playing"**—Trauma from childhood abuse can lead a person as an adult to play the role of the Child to some-one else playing the role of Parent. Rather than behaving as an Adult in relationships, and rather than seeking a relationship with another willing to behave as an Adult, our experience was that the abused Child will often end up in a relationship with someone with a domineering or manipulative personality who will assume the role of Parent. As an abused person, we can play a subservient role, but we can also show passive-aggressive behavior with the one playing the Parent. At other times, we drop the charade and engage in all-out fighting. Those three aspects in relationships are often dismissed as "typical addictive behavior" when in fact they are the typical behaviors of those suffering from the effects of untreated trauma. If one has been thoroughly programmed to play the role of the Child, other results follow. That person can feel he/she should be taken care rather than accept responsibility for taking care of oneself. Such programming can shape one's entire view of the world and the universe. As adults, they can be sub-missive and behave like a Child to be watched over. If that belief system dominates, we can avoid doing for ourselves those things that we can do and must do for ourselves.

While the dependent belief system that comes with unresolved trauma can leave one submissive or passive, the aggressive nature inspired by repressed abuse can remain. Then we can see how torn the adult can feel when trauma effects yet drive us through life: we are conflicted in the duality of submissive-aggressive behaviors combined with passive-aggressive behaviors. One part of us feels we should be submissive to any source of power and that we should respect all authority while another part wants to be assertive and take control and fight authority. The confusion and stress of dual-ity and incongruity only increase when living under the influence of that thought-life and those emotions which the literature told us to "cast aside." Often, living *under the influence* of remaining trauma and emotional intoxication was as bad for us as the days of living *under the influence* of booze.

k. **"Approval Seeking"**—The approval that was not given as a child can drive an adult to seek that approval or love. Eventually, narcissism can manifest as self-seeking inspires one to focus on self constantly and try to draw attention to self. When the abused child grows into an Adult, the behavior can still be common.

l. **"Internalizing"** –Despite the anger toward abusers, the tendency of a child is nevertheless to "become" that person (similar to the "Stockholm Syndrome" mentioned earlier.) The end result of internalizing another person in that we basically become that person. (So we hear, "I'll never be like my father," but that person eventually ends up being just like his father.)

m. **"Idealizing"**—Also related to "Internalizing" and to "Deluding" is "Idealizing." The abused child can grow into an Adult who idealizes. For example, one might heard an idealization such as "My parents didn't have much money or education, but I have to say that they did one heck of a job." (Can one hear the ego driving such a comment as well? We can also idealize about ourselves.) Or, "that person is perfect for me" or "My child is the best kid in the world," or "My lover is the greatest person in the world," though behaviors indicate the opposite.

n. **"Betraying"**—Just as abused children often become adults who abuse, so children betrayed as children can become betrayers as adults. We can betray others in relationships, we can betray people we are in business with, and we can betray ourselves by continuing to be driven to self-destruct.

o. **"Magical Thinking"**—Magical thinking becomes an outgrowth of earlier "Escapism," "A Desire for Power," and "Delusion." One step to being free of the hidden effects of stored trauma that drive us and inspired our addictions is to see that our emotional development was arrested and that we therefore often act in a childish manner. On occasion, our reasoning and conduct represent that of a very immature child. We even say that we're "a teen in an adult body" or "a child with a grownup's body."

The "magical" thinking in children—hoping for an entity with power to show up in our lives and save us—translates into delusional, magical thinking as adults. Adults who use magical thinking will assign blame and/or cause for the events in their lives to some longed-for power. They often become obsessed with gaining power, with having control via power, and with having power at their beck-and-call. They will even worship what they believe to be the source of their power—be it money or mates or muscles; in fact, the power can be conceived of in more ways than can be listed, so skillful is the mind at dreaming up sources that can offer desired power. One can see that the alcoholic's obsessive mind and his obsession with controlling, obsessing with self, obsessing with bodily comfort, obsessing with desiring to escape anything painful, and with obsessing over getting power are all rooted in childhood fantasies that can continue with magical thinking even as an adult.

p. **"Dissociating"**—Another trait fostered in childhood trauma that can plague adults is dissociation. Because of the mental, emotional, and physical pain associated with the abuse of the body, a defense mechanism triggers. The abused child will begin to disassociate from the body…will stop allowing things to be felt. Mentally, the child will "go away." Physically, the child tunes out the body's natural signals that indicate pain and suffering. As an adult, the dissociation can continue and the adult ignores the pains that result from abuse. Often, we did not experience the alarms that were being set off by our bodies and minds. Adults with dissociation will not recognize their own depression that others see clearly; they have a high tolerance for self-induced pain. They cannot see their often insane, destructive behavior. They lose touch with cause and effect associations. They become dominated by denial.

q. **"Avoiding Intimacy, Avoiding Touch"**–Trauma survivors who suffered so much from physical abuse involving touching often recoil as adults at the touch. In some cases, the abuse manifested as a tender touch; in other cases, the abuse came as a violent touch. People abused in this manner can, later on as adults, find romantic adventure appealing but are unavailable for the intimacy of romance itself. To "let go" or to commit fully no longer comes naturally.

r. **"Avoiding Attachment/Commitment, Detachment Disorder"**–While we knew that attachments that result in dependencies were unhealthy, we learned how unhealthy Detachment Disorder can be. The adult who was traumatized as a child often experiences relationship problems based in her/his inability to commit. One might say, "I like to be held, to cuddle." An adult suffering "Attachment Disorder might answer, "You're too demanding" or "I'm tired. Just let me rest." Adults with this disorder find it difficult to make commitments, and if they do make commitments, they often find it difficult to keep the commitments they made. Mates or partners of people suffering from Attachment Disorder often feel rejected.

s. **"Carrying Shame"**—Trauma survivors carry multiple loads of shame. Shame can inspire one to avoid the treatment needed to truly get to the deepest levels of pain and then to face them and release them. Those who have been abused carry multiple loads of shame. First, the perpetrator is shamed by his/her actions and dumps that shame on the abused. The abused also feels his/her own shame as a result of the abuse incidents. Wrongly carrying multiple loads of shame can inspire one to refuse to seek treatment, to repress all memory of the abuse, or to hold back in treatment rather than face all of the elements that need to be faced. Shame bearers then project the shame to others.

One can see a recurring pattern in all of the behaviors associated with untreated trauma: they cycle. The sufferer becomes a source of suffering for others. The effects of abuse are passed on, received and absorbed for another, and then passed on again. The cycle can be broken when proper and effective treatment is received and releases the negative energy that is stored at a cellular level.

EMOTIONAL HEALING, EMOTIONAL SOBRIETY: TREATING TRAUMA

If any of the above aspects of trauma become evident in one's life, then further treatment might be indicated. A major part of the work that moved Mark and me toward emotional sobriety was the treatment that we have undergone for the remaining impact of trauma. Some told me to "get over it and move on." Would that it might be that simple, but our experience was that a multi-level, holistic approach had to be used to address adequately all aspects of the four-levels of healing which Bill W. discussed and that we needed.

Research now shows that if one has an addictive personality, the odds are great that one has suffered trauma. The incidence of trauma leading to addiction is *that* prevalent. If one's trauma has not been treated specifically, the possibility is significant that it is still unresolved and is thus driving the person's subconscious thought-life and thus his conscious beliefs and thus his behaviors. And if new trauma is being experienced as an adult, it is often linked to the childhood trauma that has yet been untreated. In another of his books, Floyd described an encounter with a physical therapist who worked with his neck and back pains years after an auto accident. The therapist described the way that animals work out the effects of trauma that would otherwise remain stored in every cell of the body and the way that humans are raised *not* to release the trauma effects. The therapist in Floyd's other book explained

...all living creatures on earth, if they survive such trauma, undergo the release process. All except humans. We're told to 'get a grip,' and 'fight the tears.' Only those humans who missed the Anglo programming in this culture can absolutely let the pain flow out. They are the ones you see crying convulsively, and when others who are programmed see the convulsive reaction and are uncomfortable with a show of their own emotions, they hate this show of feelings as well. So they go right into action, doing everything they can to try to persuade the suffering person from doing what is natural. They will use all means of persuasion to try to interrupt the release of the trauma-energy. If they fail to release that energy," he continued, *"then those persons will find themselves like you, on this table, on your back. They'll be calling on me to treat their backaches, or their headaches, or their neck aches. They'll be strapped to surgery tables, needlessly in many cases, willing to allow someone to cut out parts because their trauma was never released naturally. This is the heritage passed along to most in this culture, that Saxon 'shut-up-and-be-a-big-boy-or-a-big-girl' nonsense that restricts them, makes then rigid, cold, capable of expressing emotions like anger and rage but incapable of experiencing any true feel-*

ings. The pain I'm addressing in you, though the injury happened twenty years ago, is triggered by the mental, by the stored memories that yet lie at the cellular level. It is your pain-body and mind-body, working against you. It is your upbringing working against you; it is all the crap that you were told in the past that is working against you." (from **The Twice-Stolen Necklace Murders, pp. 69-70**)

The founders used teams of professional to help address the grave emotional and mental disorders being suffered by most who came their way. They knew that "psychologists and doctors and specialists of varied kinds" were often needed to address these effects after the step work had been completed. They stated that precisely in the literature. Eventually, the need for additional work in the area of the emotions led both Mark and me to trauma specialists who use an experiential approach to treat the traumatic effects of repressed, unresolved trauma. We eventually expanded upon that treatment and benefited from a holistic approach to addressing our remaining P.T.S.D. effects as well. The changes that came have been of a whole new level and variety, uncovering much of what inspired us to develop an addictive personality in the first place. Our additional actions led us toward the state of emotional sobriety that Bill W. introduced to us.

Another action that helped free us of the influence of that "child" within was (a) to admit its influence was there, even though we might be in an adult body and (b) to declare our independence from that "child." To be able to declare that independence did not come by choosing to do so. It came after receiving professional help from a trauma specialist team. In my case, the declaration manifested first at a cellular level before I was then able to declare it consciously.

If you so chose to share in the action I took, you may turn to the Workbook at the end of this book, find APPENDIX TEN, and read out loud the declaration that came after my trauma treatment. Read it time and again if you choose, but know that even more than declaring one's freedom is required. Such was our experience anyway. The declaration was not my treatment. It is what I realized and was finally able to verbalize as a result of being freed from the trauma that was stored at the deepest level within me. If you can relate to the words, then it might be that you could benefit from someone with expert knowledge in treating trauma sufferers. If full freedom does not come, then our experience showed that there is no shame in seeking professional help. In fact, we give great credit to those who seek every avenue needed for full recovery.

The "Magical Thinking" discussed earlier—which leads to delusional thinking among adults—is another source of emotional intoxication that I experienced even as an adult. Expecting magical things to come to me, rather than doing those things that I must do for myself, often left me confused and disappointed and even angry. The irritation and puzzlement came after my expectation of magical intervention failed to materialize. I was told by a sponsor that no one and no God would do for me what I could do for myself. Peace came when I took the action to seek the additional treatment that I required to be free of the trauma influences that were still triggering emotional intoxication.

More relief from emotional intoxication came when I learned that emotions are the reactions of ego-states to perceived threats. Since ego-states are based in the delusions of false identities, then part of the treatment required to prevent emotional intoxication is the trauma-work that frees us of delusional thinking and helps restore us to sanity. We see truth, and we stop assigning blame to mysterious entities and we stop assigning credit to imagined sources. We see reality; in fact, we see The Great Reality. That was my experience.

CHAPTER 27

Thus ends Mark and Floyd's story for now of their experiences with "A Twelve-Step Journey to *SELF*-Transformation" as well as "The Other Steps" required afterwards for them to reach all four levels of sobriety. The results of the extra steps impacted in a major fashion that "man on the couch," that "man on the tape." The same result came through the extra steps taken by that "man on the bed who heard a tape" which began a process that has transformed him completely.

And where they thought they had reached a zenith after their life-changing journey through the steps, it would be "The Other Steps" that further healed their bodies, minds and emotions. The additional treatment shifted them to a higher level of happiness and joy and peace than ever experienced before. Very clear in their minds, however, is the fact they would *never* have taken "The Other Steps" without having worked exactly as outlined in the literature *The First Twelve* Steps; therefore, they will never minimize the necessity, nor the benefits, of working those first twelve. They are the primary requirement. Nothing good would have ever come without having completed those steps first.

But along the way, the man on the couch and the man on the bed became tremendously grateful for learning in time that more was required in their case. They often think back to an earlier point: *Scientists speak of parallel universes. Geometry talks of parallel lines—lines running an equal distance apart at all points and never touching. Sometimes there are distant lives that seem to run a parallel course. Occasionally…they just happen to touch.* The two lives touched and the men took together the twelve steps that began the changes in them both.

Later, as they knew more healing was needed even after all their spiritual efforts, some other lives touched theirs. Those people had been professionally-trained to bring healing not just to the spirit but to the body and to the mind and to the emotions. If you sense that a holistic treatment is required to give you full and final and complete recovery, the hope of Mark and Floyd is that you follow the literature's suggestion and search until such lives touch yours. May you find *all* of the healers that your spirit and body and mind and emotions require; may you find Your True *SELF*; and may you then enjoy the peace that will manifest after reaching *all four levels of sobriety* and knowing Your True *SELF*.

CHAPTER 28

"EPILOGUE"

The events described in "Part One" took place during the Spring of 1997. Before that time, Floyd only *thought* that he had worked the steps. Since that event, the two took "The Other Steps" alluded to in this book. The authors today continue their holistic approach to healing, and that approach includes another key element as well: financial counseling to create "Financial Sobriety."

Mark made the point that he had…**sought financial counsel and was encouraged to look at the belief systems I had been taught to see how ineffective they were and to commit to changes in my monetary life.** The two booklets that outlined the plan and helped shape new beliefs about money are available. The content of two booklets resulted in his sane and sound ideal around money, and that shifted him to a higher state of fiscal responsibility. They are entitled **"Living Within Your Means"** and **"Ending Financial Problems by Understanding Your Personality Type."** Both are available through either Mark or Floyd's websites listed below.

Mark and Floyd will be releasing two co-authored volumes in 2005, one entitled **Give Me Your Hand—Feel My Scars**, addressing their experience with healing trauma in order to heal relationships. The other work is entitled **Daily Meditations** from **A Twelve-Self Journey to SELF-Transformation.** The authors found that, in their case, a period of time early each day—spent in contemplation and consideration—resulted in benefits throughout the day. For them, *contemplation* follows the strict definition of "surveying visually or mentally" while *consideration* encompasses all that the definition implies: "careful thought, deliberation, reflection, and study." To find more about Mark and his books, you are invited to visit his website at www.MarkDHouston.com. Floyd has written a sequel to this work. You may read his account of what followed afterwards as he transitioned into The Great Reality and the knowing of Who He Really Is in a book that his publisher called *"A New Genre: 'Self-Help' and 'Personal Growth' in a Mystery-Romance Format."* That book, released in early 2004, is entitled **The Twice-Stolen Necklace Murders** and is available at www.FloydHenderson.com. For now, may you go in peace.

PART FIVE

THE WORKBOOK

APPENDIX ONE

(Affirming the Third Step Decision)

The literature says that **"the wording is optional"**
for the Third Step Decision. We offer a modified version
that a group member received from Clarence S.
—similar to what Dr. Bob used with him.

I am calling on my Creative Intelligence within that I've ignored for years. I've made a mess of my life by allowing the subconscious mind to guide me. I want to turn away from all the wrong things I've ever done and all the wrong things I've ever been. I know there's a power within that can change my life and can turn things around for me. I am grateful I've lived long enough—despite the efforts of my ego to kill me—to become interested in trying to find another way to live.

I commit to working the rest of the steps in order to kill off the ego and to learn how to tap into the Higher Power within so I can get sane guidance throughout my days. I am making this conscious decision to turn my will and my life over to the care and control of another Guide, another Manager.

I ask that awareness of that resource within move into my being and make itself real inside me and fill my awful emptiness. Fill me with a consciousness of the spirit within and make me know the will of my Higher Power for me. I am also ready to learn how to test my thoughts to see if they are from my Universal Mind or from my destructive ego.

I rejoice that I have been made aware of the existence of that Higher Power within that I can learn to use. May I be successful in working the rest of the steps so I can eliminate ego and tap into the sane part of my mind. Let it be.

APPENDIX TWO

Column One I resent or hold a grudge against:	Column Two 3 or 4 words that describe the person, institution or rule are:			
_____	_____	_____	_____	_____
_____	_____	_____	_____	_____
_____	_____	_____	_____	_____
_____	_____	_____	_____	_____
_____	_____	_____	_____	_____

APPENDIX THREE

(Affirming the Seventh Step Decision)

I am acknowledging all my past wrongs and all my defects of character. I want to start a new life today, and I am grateful for seeing the lies that I believed which held me back and for seeing the truth that can set me free.

I ask that my resource within, which I have neglected in the past, awaken now and guide my life. I'm grateful for this opportunity to wipe my slate clean and start my life anew. In Steps Four, Five and Six I have completed my moral inventory and I have admitted to myself and another person the exact nature of my wrongs. I now admit these wrongs to my Higher Power and invoke it to reject every single defect of character, now and in the future.

I am grateful for a chance to be a part of the solutions in life instead of the problems. I invoke my Higher Power to grant me wisdom, knowledge and strength as I go out from here to live the life of happiness that I am capable of enjoying if I allow my Right Mind to guide me.

I am grateful for the steps that will teach me to set aside my wrong thinking and give me the tools necessary for tapping into my Creative Intelligence. Let it be.

APPENDIX FOUR

Steps 4 and 5 may leave certain areas uncovered that yet need review. Use of the following guide will allow you to uncover any remaining shortcomings that have caused you and others so much trouble. We must find our part in those troubles. Part of the guide will help you bring those beliefs to the conscious part of your mind and address them, to see where they are causing you problems and to afford you the opportunity to ask The Higher Power Within to direct your thinking so that your assets (instead of your defects) will dominant your life. The guide will also help you see where you have been driven by ego to cause problems for yourself and others. Finally, the literature says that some of our troubles are caused by our "fallacious reasoning," so the guide will help you uncover certain errors in the way we alcoholics think.

Our egos do not like an honest inventory and ego will fight for its life with such thoughts as, "I know, but..." or "Yeah, but...." Having worked with thousands of alcoholics has proved time and again that there are twenty defects most of us alcoholics have in common—and that most people in the world have—that make up the nature of human wrongs and which lead to our problems. In alcoholics, the defects are often expressed to a magnified degree. The truth is that these twenty defects are the result of wrong, insane thinking. To be certain that we do not overlook any of our defects that we'll want removed, let's see how many, in all honesty, we can identify. *Please mark in the second column any of the liabilities you can now see have been a part of your life:*

FOURTH STEP MORAL INVENTORY

ASSETS (Positives)	LIABILITIES (Negatives)
1. Forgiveness	1. Resentment / Anger / Judging
2. Love / Loving	2. Fear / Being Opinionated
3. Self-Forgetfulness	3. Self-Pity / Whining
4. Humility	4. Self-Justification
5. Modesty	5. Self-Importance / Egotism

6. Self-Valuation	6. Self-Condemnation / Guilt
7. Honesty	7. Lying / Evasion / Dishonesty
8. Patience	8. Impatience
9. Unpretentiousness	9. Pride / Phoniness /Denial
10. Trust	10. Uncertainty / Jealousy
11. Satisfaction	11. Envy/Craving/Need/Want
12. Activity / Industriousness	12. Laziness/ Seeker of Shortcuts
13. Promptness	13. Procrastination /Inconsiderate
14. Straightforwardness	14. Insincerity
15. Positive Thinking	15. Negative Thinking
16. Spiritual(Sane) Thinking	16. Immoral (Insane) Thinking
17. Tolerance/Not Controlling	17. Intolerance/ Controlling
18. Praise for Others	18. Criticism/Loose Talk / Gossip
19. Calm / Silent	19. Go-er/Doer/Zoomer/Talker
20. Generous	20. Greed / Faithlessness

We invite you to look at the assets column now and know that those are available to you. We all have those within us, ready to emerge, but the liabilities (which are their exact opposite) suppress them. Be heartened by the fact that those are going to emerge at the end of this work. Look forward to seeing those assets manifest.

Now, our founders made clear that the Fifth Step asks us to look for the "nature" of our wrongs at this point, not all our wrongs. They also knew that we could never be happy, joyous and free unless we see *our part* in the troubles in our lives. We invite you now to look at another set of liabilities that we exhibited in the past that also blocked off other assets. These liabilities, when they manifested, separated us from our Real *SELF* and from The Higher Power Within and from others. We needed to review carefully all of our **belief systems** to uncover the defects in our thinking and behavior that they caused.

AREA ONE IS "BELIEF SYSTEMS THAT RESULT IN CHARACTER DEFECTS"

(List in each blank an example when you displayed each)

1. **Selfishness**: Caring too much for oneself and too little for others; showing care solely for oneself; not feeling concerned that I have ruined the lives of others.

_____

2. **Judging**: Criticizing or evaluating others when they have not given consent to do so.

_____

3. **Projecting**: Trying to predict future events; believing that current conditions are a guaranteed indicator of future events.

_____

4. **Rejection of Self**: Considering oneself as useless or vile; having low self-esteem; believing oneself unworthy.

_____

5. **Inadequacy**: Believing you are defective, insufficient, or not equal to the task or the purpose.

_____

6. **Envy**: Discontented or excited by the sight of another's superiority or success; a feeling that makes a person begrudge another for his good fortune.

_____

7. **Jealousy**: Mental uneasiness because of suspicion or fear or rivalry.

_____

8. **Impatience**: Restlessness; intolerance of delay; expecting or demanding immediate gratification.

9. **Impulsiveness**: Tending to act impetuously; making hasty decisions; swayed by emotional or involuntary impulses.

10. **Oversensitivity**: Being easily shocked, offended, or irritated—to the extreme.

11. **Procrastination**: Putting off from day to day, delaying; putting off to some future time.

12. **Dependence**: A state of relying upon another for emotional or physical support, existence, or well-being.

13. **Worry**: Tormenting oneself with, or suffering from, disturbing thoughts.

14. **Indecisiveness**: Being unable to make decisions; hesitating when action would be appropriate.

15. **Isolation**: Separation from others; cutting oneself off from contact with others.

16. **Self Pity**: Feeling pain or grief for oneself; suffering that is exacerbated by one's own distress. This developed in some of us because we were raised in abusive homes and the abuse sometimes was halted when we were sick. Also, if there were things we were afraid to do or simply did not want to do, we could feign sickness and escape doing it and also get some kind attention, maybe. Now,

we carry such silliness and game-playing into our adulthood and our adult relations and try to manipulate others with it.

17. **Perfectionism**: A personal philosophy that demands flawlessness in both others and oneself. (Consider the link with Procrastination)

18. **False Pride**: Having an unreasonable opinion of one's own superiority over others; inordinate self-esteem; the reflection of this quality in disdainful or arrogant behavior.

19. **Guilt**: A feeling of remorse caused by accepting personal responsibility (real or imagined) for an offense or problem.

20. **Resentment**: A deep sense of injury; anger arising from a sense of wrong; strong displeasure.

21. **Intolerance**: Refusing to tolerate others' opinions, rights, or beliefs.

22. **Demanding**: Making authoritative requests or claims; expecting more than is normally necessary in a situation.

23. **Vengeance**: The getting even for wrong or injury; retribution; revenge.

24. **Manipulation**: Fraudulent management for one's advantage; to manage or influence by artful skill, often by unfair tactics; to

adapt or change to suit one's purpose or advantage.

---

25. **Alibis (Lying/Excuse-Making)**: Providing a fabricated excuse; claiming innocence; saying something that is intended to convey a false impression.

---

26. **Dishonesty**: The inclination to deceive, cheat; steal, embezzle, or defraud in order to gain what one wants.

---

27. **Fear**: A painful emotion caused by expectation of evil or impending danger or dread, or of not getting your wants met.

---

28. **Rebellion**: A fight or struggle against any authority or controls; exertion of self-will over all restraints, whether societal, physical, relational, legal, or otherwise.

---

29. **Controlling**: Wanting to have the power to rule, guide, or manage others; having the desire to direct or regulate people, places, things; wanting to be in charge.

AREA TWO IS "BELIEF SYSTEMS THAT RESULT FROM USE OF EGO-DEFENSIVE MECHANISMS AND THAT PRODUCE CHARACTER DEFECTS"

(LIST A TIME YOU'VE SHOWN EACH)

Psychologists for years have recognized the existence of what they call "ego-defense mechanisms": behaviors that humans practice in order to preserve and protect the ego. The mechanisms are often fear-based or lie-based and thus are considered the source of some character defects.

30. **Projection** (psychological): Unconsciously ascribing to others one's own ideas, impulses, or emotions; finding and pointing out in others the faults we subconsciously most hate in ourselves.

31. **Egotism**: The excessive use of "I," "My," "Me;" self-conceit; selfishness; narcissism; the habit of thinking, talking, or writing too much of oneself.

32. **Egocentrism**: Recognizing the self as the center of all things; self-centered; believing that everything should revolve around you and your wishes.

33. **Rejection of Others**: Casting off others or their opinions: refusing to consider others or their opinions as useful.

34. **Justification**: Furnishing a reason or excuse for one's behavior.

35. **Victimization**: ("Victim Syndrome"): The feeling of being destroyed, sacrificed, or injured by one's own distresses; blaming others for one's self-induced crises.

36. **Blame**: Placing on another person or thing the responsibility for a mistake or fault of one's own.

37. **Rationalization**: Attributing logical or credible motives for actions actually resulting from other often unrecognized (or hidden) motives; finding or creating plausible but false motives for one's conduct; making excuses for unacceptable behaviors.

38. Grandiosity: The desire to seem important; to be pompous or showy.

---

39. Excessiveness: Overindulging; being immoderate; wanting more than what is needed; wanting a quantity beyond what is necessary or desirable; wanting to exceed others.

AREA THREE IS "BELIEF SYSTEMS THAT RESULT FROM FALLACIES IN REASONING THAT PRODUCE CHARACTER DEFECTS"

(LIST A TIME YOU'VE USED EACH)

40. Abandoning Discussion: Refusing to complete discussion of issues to resolution; walking out; throwing a punch.

---

41. Affirming the Consequent: Justifying your behavior by desire only. (I want it; therefore, I can take it.)

---

42. Appeal to Pity: Trying to get one's way by practicing self-pity; suggesting to others that your condition is the most pitiful and thereby trying to get special consideration.

---

43. Personal Attack: Believing your status can be elevated by reducing the status of others.

---

44. Apriorism: Closing one's mind to the facts or one's eyes to the evidence; being prejudiced to the point of being unable to consider an opposing idea or a different opinion; an inability to learn as a result of believing you know everything.

45. **Demand for Special Consideration**: Convinced that you are different, you then believe that you deserve to be treated in a way that is different from the way that everyone else is treated.

46. **Forestalling Disagreement**: Attempting to manipulate others' beliefs and their acceptance of your beliefs; trying to block people from disagreeing with you (e.g., saying "No one would be so insane as to believe....")

47. **Impossible Condition**: Giving people several choices while none of the options are plausible ("Either do it my way or get out.")

48. **Inconsistency**: Making incompatible statements; not holding yourself to the same principles at all times.

49. **Lip Service**: Saying you are for something while your actions contradict you.

50. **Non-Exhaustive Classification**: Contradicting oneself and not recognizing it ("I don't mean to tell you how to run your business, but ....")

51. **Non-Exclusive Classification**: Using generalizations to justify your behavior.

52. **Pointing to Another Wrong**: Attempting to avoid accepting deserved criticism by deflection (*"I'm* driving dangerously? *You're* the one who nearly killed us last year on vacation.")

---

53. **Post Hoc**: Reaching erroneous conclusions. ("My father was insensitive. I'm insensitive. There's nothing I can do about it.")

---

54. **Red Herring**: Changing the subject in order to deflect attention to another issue instead of the one that is making you uncomfortable.

---

55. **Trouble with Conditionals and Alternatives**: Giving false reasons to explain events ("If life treated me fairer, I'd have a better job, better attitude, etc.")

If you have found new shortcomings or defects that you want removed, then read this aloud again:

(AFFIRMING THE SEVENTH STEP, AGAIN)

I am acknowledging all my past wrongs and all my defects of character. I want to start a new life today, and I am grateful for seeing the lies that I believed, which have held me back, and for seeing the truth that can set me free.

I ask that my resource within, which I have neglected in the past, awaken now and guide my life. I'm grateful for this opportunity to wipe my slate clean and start my life anew. In Steps Four, Five and Six I have completed my moral inventory and I have admitted to myself and another person the exact nature of my wrongs. I now admit these wrongs to my Higher Power and invoke it to reject every single defect of character, now and in the future.

I am grateful for a chance to be a part of the solutions in life instead of the problems. I invoke my Higher Power to grant me wisdom, knowledge and strength as I go out from here to live the life of happiness that I am capable of enjoying if I allow my Right Mind to guide me.

I am grateful, for the steps that will teach me to set aside my wrong thinking and give me the tools necessary for tapping into my Creative Intelligence. Let it be.

You are now the cleanest, purest person on the face of the earth. Why? Because you haven't had a chance to harm anyone or practice your defects after their removal seconds ago! Because you haven't even had a chance for even a milder form of them to show up!

Finally, we have a caution we'd like to share: your defects that allowed your self-will to run riot have been removed, but your "self" is not completely gone. Why? Because your *mind*, the subconscious part that controls what you *do*, has not been completely changed. It still contains a lot of old ideas and beliefs and you have not yet developed the skills necessary to go to the second (opposite) thought which comes when we allow The Higher Power Within—the Universal Mind—to guide us totally. We only get that result by doing Step 11 every morning and throughout the day. Also, your ego/self remains in tact until you finish Steps 8 and 9 and you make *all* amends. Therefore, conflict *will* manifest within you: your ego *will* fight with your Right Mind. But there is good news: our experience shows that conflict precedes clarity; however, your thought-life will only change when you do steps 8 and 9 thoroughly and commence working Steps 10, 11, and 12 at the same time on a daily basis. You are changed now, but you cannot be content ever again unless you do the remainder of the work in Steps 8 to 12, so we'll see you at the next meeting.

APPENDIX FIVE

Write the <u>names</u> only, then we'll decide together what <u>actions</u> are called for. Remember, you agreed to go to any length to get a better life, so we need to be thorough and list *every* person or institution we harmed. Take a few minutes and list each name that comes to mind in the different categories:

EIGHT STEP LIST
Names of relatives   Action:
I've had problems with:

_____
_____
_____
_____
_____
_____
_____

Names of employees/employers   Action:
I've had problems with:

_____
_____
_____
_____

Names of agencies/institutions   Action:
I've had problems with:

_____
_____
_____
_____

Names of laws/rules Action:
I've had problems with:

_____

_____

_____

_____

Names of people/businesses Action:
I owe money:

_____

_____

_____

_____

APPENDIX SIX

EVENING REVIEW QUESTIONS

Was I resentful at any time today? Selfish? Dishonest? Afraid?
Do I owe an apology? Do I need to discuss something with someone at once? Was I kind? What could I have done better? Was I
thinking of self or of others?

APPENDIX SEVEN

GUIDE TO MEDITATION AND GUIDANCE

[Say]: "In my Right Mind, I realize that the people who
wronged me are sick people, just as I was. I intend to set my ego
aside now and seek to give them the same tolerance, pity, and
patience that I would cheerfully grant a sick friend. I seek now to
become conscious of where I have been selfish, self-seeking, dishonest or fear-based, thus causing my own trouble. To maintain

peace of mind, I now admit that I do not have to retaliate and I admit that I am not a victim.

"I ask the Higher Power within to relieve me of all my fears, worries, and doubts and turn over all decision-making to the Right Mind within.

"In all my relations, I ask for inner guidance to take over. Give me a vision of a sane and sound ideal in my sex relations, and let me imagine what might happen in my life were I able to move closer to the ideal I have been trying to glimpse. Allow me to take the action to restore sanity around my spending habits as well. Let me be reminded that the universe intended life to be simple and that I should keep it the way the universe made it. I will keep it real simple by releasing to my Right Mind all decision-making today."

Early members in the fellowship recommended daily readings of what they called "Power Phrases." These are phrases that seemingly make no sense when we first read them. So what is the rationale behind them?

RATIONALE

We are looking for *original* thoughts, for a different way of thinking and perceiving. We have been thinking like the masses and following a path that was not true to our Real *SELF*. We're not trying to isolate or separate ourselves, but we are trying to place some mental distance between the rat-race mentality and our new sense of peace that we want to maintain. So how do we build that space? We are attempting to affirm the Power within, not our past weaknesses. We have found that if we are to experience the necessary psychic change, the phrases provided will help you develop a new way of thinking, a way that is different from the perspective of the masses that are trapped in the going and doing and zooming of the ego. These phrases can give us a new and different perspective if we internalize them:

I will have no expectations nor make demands today
What I resist persists
I will cease fighting
I can resist nothing today while still standing up for my own

Highest Good

I do not have the power to drive anyone crazy or to make anyone sane. Each individual is responsible for her/his own peace of mind

It is none of my business what anyone thinks about me or about anything else...it's my business what I think about them

I do not have the power to make anyone stay in my life

I do not have the power to drive anyone away

I do not have the power to make anyone miserable

I do not have the power to make anyone happy

I will love all

I do not have to like all

My goal is peace of mind (also known as "sanity" or "spiritual living")

The only way I can forgive someone today is to think I am "Their Judge" and "Their Forgiver"; I and the world will be better off if I do not judge in the first place

I do not know what is "good" or "bad," and everything ultimately works out for the best when my perspective is truthful

The Higher Power will take charge when I let go

I do not need to know anything or understand anything but instead will only seek The Higher Power's guidance, which I receive intuitively if I become still and quiet

I will not wish, hope, want, desire, nor crave today

I will not pursue love—I will simply give love

I cannot be content *in* a relationship until I am content *without* a relationship

I will think less and employ intuition more

The past is gone—it's an image in my mind

The future can be no more than an image in my mind

Therefore, the present moment is the only real moment; I shall not allow false images to affect the way I feel

Next, we are going to give you some key phrases that have proved effective in changing wrong thinking. If we say them enough, we *will* change our thinking patterns. Try working these comments into your thought-life and vocabulary throughout the day, for each is intended to reverse the faulty thinking that made us miserable in the past:

"Everything really is going to be OK." (Why say that? Because we have always lived by the motto: "Nothing is gonna be alright!")

"I love this." Because we hated everything in the past, every time something bothers you today you say immediately, "I love this." Then ask, "Why?" and come up with a reason. (Think of a reason why you'll not only accept it but love it. "I just got fired. I love this. Why? Because the universe has a better job for me. I didn't like this job anyway.")

"Whatever." (We say this with acceptance, not with a sense of not caring anymore. Why use this one? Because we could never accept anything that went contrary to what our egos thought we wanted or needed.)

"I must get rid of that belief, unlearning something I was taught that was wrong." (Remember that we have belief systems given us by others. We have to set them aside to receive new thoughts originating in our Creative Intelligence.)

"I have no opinion to express about that." (Why use this? Because our egos always had an opinion to express on every topic. We had to show off how much we knew, how informed we were. Our narcissism also drove us to have and to express an opinion on everything. And no one cared. They still don't want to hear it, so we work on keeping our opinions to ourselves now.)

"I will not judge anyone today; I will not criticize today." (In the past we have been some of the most judgmental, critical people on the planet. That builds negative energy. We are looking for positive energy. We have no idea what experiences people have undergone that make them the way they are. We need to realize that most things we had an opinion about, that we judged people about, were really none of our business and really didn't matter in the least.)

"I will not whine and think I'm a victim today." (Self-pity is our enemy. We've been the cause of most of our problems, but we like to blame others. Today, we are seeking our part in any problem and we cannot find our part when we imagine we are being victimized. If we have been a victim of abuse, we should seek treatment for that.)

APPENDIX EIGHT

RESENTMENT INVENTORY— "PEOPLE"-FORM "A"

COLUMN ONE:
NAME_____

COLUMN TWO: What's wrong with this person that angers / troubles me (Name 3 things, such as: "selfish," "manipulative," "controlling," "dishonest," "a jerk," "a nag," "hit me," "abandoned me," "stole my stuff," etc.):
1._____
2._____
3._____

COLUMN THREE: Seven areas where this affects me:
1. <u>Self-esteem:</u> I am (or see myself as):_____

2. <u>Pride:</u> No one should see the following being done to me:
_____

3. <u>Ambition:</u> What I want but think I'm losing is
_____

4. <u>Emotional Security:</u> To feel OK, I need
_____

5. <u>Financial Security:</u> My financial security is threatened in this deal because_____

6. <u>Relations (by Sex)</u>:
I think *men* should_____
I think *women* should_____

7. <u>Personal Relations:</u> Those close to me should see that I am

_____

COLUMN FOUR: My part in this incident is that I was...
a. *Selfish* (I want to keep what I have, so here's how I was selfish):

_____

b. *Self-Seeking* (I also want what others have, so here's where I
was *seeking* for my *self*):_____

c. *Dishonest* (The real truth is that...):_____

d. *Fear* (What I'm really worried about or afraid of
that is driving me to behave the way I'm behaving is):

_____

e. *Insanity* (Here are the things about my behavior and feelings
that are really insane in this
deal):_____

RESENTMENT INVENTORY — "PEOPLE"-FORM "B"

COLUMN ONE:
*NAME*_____

*COLUMN TWO: (I depended on this person in these areas and
this person failed me in these ways):*
1._____
2._____
3._____

COLUMN THREE: Seven areas where this affects me:
1. <u>Self-esteem:</u> (In terms of building my self-esteem, I expected

this person to):_____

2. Pride: (In terms of building my pride, I expected this person to):_____

3. Ambition: (I expected this person to provide the following that I want or need):_____

4. Emotional Security: (To feel OK, I needed for this person to):

_____

5. Financial Security: (I expected to gain the following benefits if in relationship with this person):

_____

(or, when I take care of someone's financial needs, I expect the following from them):_____

6. Relations by Sex: (When I give myself to another and have sex with them, I expect): _____

7. Personal Relations: (In dealing with them, I expect this from):
1. friends_____
2. lovers_____
3. family_____
COLUMN FOUR: (The REAL truth) My part in this problem was:
a. *Selfish* (Here's how the above reveals I was selfish):

_____

b. *Self-Seeking* (Here's how the above shows I was *seeking* more for myself than giving to another):

_____

c. Dishonest (Here's where I ....
deceived him/her):_____
(deceived myself) _____

d. *Fear* (Deals with *wrong thinking in my head* about fears, worries, insecurities that drive me. Here's where <u>my</u> thinking was wrong):_____

RESENTMENT INVENTORY—
"Principles/Rules/Laws"

COLUMN ONE:
NAME_____

COLUMN TWO: What's wrong with this rule that angers / troubles me is:
1._____
2._____
3._____

COLUMN THREE: Seven areas where this affects me:
1. <u>Self-esteem:</u> I am (or see myself as):_____

2. <u>Pride:</u> No one should see the following being done to me:
_____

3. <u>Ambition:</u> What I want but think I'm losing is
_____

4. <u>Emotional Security:</u> To feel OK, I need
_____

5. <u>Financial Security:</u> My financial security is threatened in this deal because_____

6. <u>Relations (by Sex):</u>
I think *men* should_____
I think *women* should_____

7. <u>Personal Relations:</u> Those close to me should see that I am:
_____

COLUMN FOUR: My part in this incident is that I was:

a. *Selfish* (I want to keep what I have, so here's how I was selfish): _____

b. *Self-Seeking* (I also want what others have, so here's where I was *seeking* for my *self*):_____

c. *Dishonest* (The real truth is that...):_____

d. *Fear* (What I'm really worried about or afraid of that is driving me to behave the way I'm behaving is):_____

e. *Insanity* (Here are the things about my behavior and feelings that are really insane in this deal):_____

RESENTMENT INVENTORY — "INSTITUTIONS"

COLUMN ONE:
NAME_____

COLUMN TWO: What's wrong with this institution that angers / troubles me:
1._____
2._____
3._____

COLUMN THREE: Seven areas where this affects me:
1. Self-esteem: I am (or see myself as):_____

2. Pride: No one should see the following being done to me:

_____

3. Ambition: What I want but think I'm losing is_____

4. <u>Emotional Security:</u> To feel OK, I need _____

5. <u>Financial Security:</u> My financial security is threatened in this deal because_____

6. <u>Relations (by Sex):</u>
I think *men* should_____
I think *women* should_____

7. <u>Personal Relations:</u> Those close to me should see that I

_____

COLUMN FOUR: My part in this incident is that I was:
a. *Selfish* (I want to keep what I have, so here's how I was selfish):

_____

b. *Self-Seeking* (I also want what others have, so here's where I was *seeking* for my *self*):_____

c. *Dishonest* (The real truth is that...):

_____

d. *Fearful* (What I'm really worried about or afraid of that is driving me to behave the way I'm behaving is):

_____

e. *Insane* (Here are the things about my behavior and feelings that are really insane in this deal):

_____

INVENTORY SUMMARY

Here's how I was inconsiderate:

_____

Here's how I aroused jealousy :

_____

Here's how I aroused suspicion :

_____

Here's how I aroused bitterness :

_____

Even though another may have played a part, this is <u>my</u> inventory, so here's how I was at fault:

_____

Here's what I should have done instead:

_____

My sane and sound ideal for the future, should anything similar come up again, is to:

_____

APPENDIX NINE

A 20-DAY QUICK-GROWTH PLAN

(IT IS SUGGESTED THAT EACH BEGIN THIS 20-DAY EXERCISE ON THE DAY FOLLOWING COMPLETION OF THE MEETING ON STEPS 10-12)

Practicing any addiction is self-destructive. It also drove us to harm or destroy others. How can we stop the harmful or self-destructive behaviors which had become our habit? By taking actions to form new habits and by being constructive with ourselves and with others. The intent of this exercise is to eliminate the destructive and to incorporate the constructive.

PUTTING THE PLAN INTO ACTION

You are invited to do the numbered items below for the next twenty days. Do the activity all day. If we do these things, at the end of twenty days we will be different. We will be emitting a positive energy that will attract positive energy to us, and that energy will replace the negatives that our negative liabilities have attracted. Our founders spoke not just of our liabilities but also of our assets; therefore, the exercise will allow you to practice each of the twenty asset-behaviors. If you do that, you will be a new person and you will love your new *SELF*. You'll be behaving in a lovable manner and you will honor yourself for that change. So here's the twenty-day schedule that automatically leads us away from self-hatred or self-destructive behavior and into a state of Self-Love:

Day 1: Practice forgiving others, all day long.
Day 2: Consciously catch yourself each time you start to judge someone, and stop. You won't have to worry about forgiving if you don't judge in the first place.
Day 3: Every time today you start to think about yourself, stop.
Day 4: Today—be humble. Say "I don't know" and "I have no opinion about that" and "You may be right."
Day 5: Be modest. Do not talk about yourself even once today.

Turn all conversation toward others.

Day 6: Look at yourself honestly and see the improvement already occurring. *Like* yourself for the progress. Don't beat yourself up if you don't do something perfectly.

Day 7: Be honest, all day long, but do not injure others' feelings in the process.

Day 8: Be patient. Let others go ahead of you all day.

Day 9: Be plain today. Buy nothing as a luxury. Eat modestly.

Day 10: Begin to formulate a budget that will allow you to live within your means.

Day 11: All day today, feel satisfied. Sense that what you have is enough. Say it: "I really have enough."

Day 12: Work diligently today. Put in a full day's effort. If you have no paying work, work out physically, doing something positive for your body.

Day 13: Be early. Leave the house early. Leave extra time for everything. Do not try to put 10 pounds of potatoes into a 5-pound bag.

Day 14: Be direct with people. Tell them what you are feeling, in a pleasant way. Be honest without hurting. Try being intimate in a conversation with someone.

Day 15: Create positive thoughts today. Each time something negative comes to mind, picture something positive. Think of a favorite, isolated scene and see yourself there. Replace negative thoughts with positive mental pictures and images.

Day 16: Test every thought and word and deed today to see how sane it is, asking: "Is this thought, word or deed self-constructive or self-destructive?" Seek the opposite thought to see if it might be the sane thought. (Ex.: "I'm going to go in and tell the boss to shove this job." An opposite thought: "I think I'll get another job before I quit the one I have.")

Day 17: Do not try to control anyone today. Leave everyone alone to have their own growth experience, even if you think it's crazy. Tell no one anything that they should do.

Day 18: Praise everyone you talk to today. Comment on something positive you see in them or their work or their attitude. Find something good to say to them.

Day 19: Today, be generous. Give away things all day: your time, your attention, something you value, your place in line. Help someone.

Day 20: Today, be calm and silent. Then, try it tomorrow. Then the next day. Then for a week. Then for a month. Then for a year. Then, *ad infinitum*. While others practice the freedom of speech that we brag about in the west, practice the freedom of silence that many respect in the east.

Now, a final point. Some ask: "Isn't false pride, ego, the downfall of humanity?" Yes. "So shouldn't we avoid Self-Love?" some have asked. No! Ego has been our problem all along, but Self-Love is the opposite of ego. Ego loves the false-self-images we had of ourselves in the past. Self-Love is Love of the Real *SELF*, the Real *Us* that was nothing more than a potentiality that never matured. The Real *SELF* is what we had the potential to be all along but we weren't because of the influence of being raised in an insane culture. We were destructively driven by three things that the literature tells us to cast aside: ideas, emotions, and attitudes. The Real *SELF*, which is lovable, will now come into being after twenty days of practicing asset-behaviors rather than liability-behaviors. Some will look at these twenty asset-behaviors and call their use "spiritual living." Others will call it "sane living." Whatever. We invite you to forget all labels and all analysis. Just enjoy the New, Real You. The world will.

APPENDIX TEN

"MY DECLARATION OF INDEPENDENCE FROM A TRAUMATIZED CHILD"

ABOUT THE CHILD:

The abused child remains inside the adult and can appear to you in but one way: in the form of internal dialogue. That child tries to take over. It will try to take you back to the age of traumatization and inspire you to behave like a child rather than a mature adult. It will try to inspire you to reenact past, traumatic events with a hope of bringing about a different outcome—leaving you in a state of wishing, hoping, and longing...but never happy. He will try to get you to assume guilt or shame. In the twisted world of trauma, he will try to convince you again that what is most comfortable is to live out a thought-life filled with harmful thoughts and dangerous situations and chaotic relationships. He was addicted to chaos. He will try to return to that state that is more familiar. He will try to reenact by urging you to become involved with harmful, dangerous or even "exciting" people who were often also abused in their past and who now hand out abuse themselves.

Whether that child or the adult housing that child, you do not deserve to have to carry the high-maintenance bills; you did not deserve the heavy-toll; you did not deserve to have your spirit broken—whether humorously, mockingly, financially, emotionally, critically, mentally, or otherwise. For too long, that child drove the adult to behave in a childish fashion. As adults, we must be sure that the child gets no vote from now on. You can tell the child that it can hang with you for a time, but it must be silent. It cannot lead anymore, and when it wants to engage in an internal dialogue, you'll have to ask it nicely to be quiet.

The Adult You must take charge and tell the child "I'm sorry for what you went through, but I won't let you decide for me any longer. You were warped through no fault of your own and you did not deserve what you got. You always deserved love, but you cannot be in charge of me any longer."

See that all ego-states are rooted in the concepts of that child that adopted the agenda and beliefs and concepts and cruelties of totally unprepared and incompetent people who wrongly programmed him. Remember that all internal dialogue is that wounded child speaking, but behind that child was some cruel and angry and frustrated and punishing person or a depressed, shut-down, backed-up, emotionally-unavailable and cold person. Actually, those are the ones whose voices have driven you all your life, via the abused Child. How has it worked, listening to and being guided by those people and that Child all your life?

Give them no more voice. Speak for Your *SELF*. You can be free of the prison of the thoughts and concepts of a child and the many non-loving people who guided you into that prison and who guarded you and who constantly bombarded you with their expectations and demands in order to empower them and to keep you locked away. Speak up and declare your freedom and happiness by saying out loud:

I did not deserve the abuse I received at a young age, nor any abuse received as an adult; the beliefs I was given were fictional and warped and twisted. I need no longer carry the guilt.

I did not deserve the abuse that was heaped on me and I did not deserve the abuse of people trained up to seek out the abused and to further abuse them in their desire to control and to have power and to vent their repressed anger. I did not deserve abuse from people who entered the adult world with such hostility that they abused me repeatedly and could not have cared less.

But the abused become abusers, so the truth is also that the people I have abused did not deserve it either. I will get help to be free of those things driving me so that I will no longer abuse and will no longer tolerate abuse.

I shall meet those who are on the higher floors awaiting me. I will reside in the upper floors where I belong. I will care for my SELF. When chaos manifests, I will leave; if troubles are brewing with the wait staff in a restaurant, I shall turn and leave. I will not watch anything on TV that is violent or abusive to my spirit. I shall not hang with the sick.

Freed from the child who believes it deserves punishment and is not enough and is not good enough and shall never have enough and deserves no love, I can now receive love and give love without fear of it turning on me. I need not seek out abusers to reenact what I was "comfortable with," what I found to be "familiar." For a time, I will be reminded that what "feels comfortable" may be dangerous and that what feels scary or uncomfortable is likely the sane and the normal.

I allowed many people to use me, to chew me up and to spit me out. I did not deserve that. I am fortunate to be alive, to have survived it, and to be free. I am an Adult, not a child any longer. I do not need universal acceptance, understanding, or a sense of victimization and I do not desire universal acceptance, understanding, or a sense of victimization.

When the traumatized Child was in charge, I had no choice, no chance. The Child was driven by its warped or immature beliefs, concepts, dogma, and faulty conditioning. Now, I have a chance, a chance to give love freely and to receive it freely—without a need for approval, validation, or affirmation.

I am no longer striving to adapt for the sake of survival—the survival of certain ego-states inspired by a child or by this culture. I no longer have to work at adapting to abusive people or to a sick little Child. I no longer have to be driven by (or try to adopt) the sick beliefs of others. I no longer have to be frustrated by the unrealistic expectations and the constant demands of others. I do not have to play the Child to someone else playing the Parent in my relationships.

I survived all my abusers and their terror, their bewildering behavior, their frustrating demands, their despair-causing cruelty, their abandonment, their disloyalty, their repressed anger, and their inability to love unconditionally. I can now separate from the Child and from those other abusers as well.

The only voice the Child and the new Adult should be given is not the voice to lead but the voice to say: "Stop it!" if others try to abuse me or use me. The Child can say, "Leave me alone. Stop messing with my head and my heart. Quit your efforts to hurt me or to abuse me or to control me or to gain a sense of empowerment through manipulating me 'with love.' Stop trying to take advantage of the helplessness I was left in because I was wounded and abused and hurt and powerless to protect myself."

And yes, the Child and new Adult can sometimes get angry and say: "Stop it, damn it! You were a user—ungrateful and uncaring. Being around you made me even sicker. Your actions regarding me do not show how 'bad' I was but how truly sick that you are. I don't want to hurt you, but I do want to stay very far away from your negativity and your coldness and your sickness and your repressed anger and your backed-up emotions. Thus, I hereby declare my freedom from all who would abuse me or treat me in a fashion less than I deserve. I declare that I shall never again submit myself to the control or to the influence of the beliefs and concepts of anyone. I declare I am free, and I do not have to return to my past mental and emotional prison ever again."

Now, go in peace.

OTHER WORKS BY MARK H. AND FLOYD H.

GIVE ME YOUR HAND—FEEL MY SCARS

(Release date: 2005)

Floyd's "sequel" to
A Twelve-Step Journey to SELF-Transformation
is

THE TWICE-STOLEN

NECKLACE MURDERS

*("A New Genre: SELF-HELP and PERSONAL GROWTH in a
Mystery-Romance Format")*

For those who want to know more, my full journey is discussed in a personal growth book entitled **The Twice-Stolen Necklace Murders**. It continues with my story from the point where this book with Mark leaves off.

SYNOPSIS OF

The Twice-Stolen Necklace Murders

This book picks up with Floyd's post-step-work and post-taking-the-other-steps journey, when new problems manifested that again challenged the positive effects gained from all his efforts and healing. As more *was disclosed*, he would reach even greater heights of peace though stripped of all that he valued so highly in his days of four-level sobriety. In some ways, the losses and the pain seemed even greater than that suffered during his drinking days. This is a discourse in how he found an even higher level of peace that came after losing it all…even while sober.

SAMPLE QUOTES FROM THE BOOK

KIRK WILDMAN ON . . .

INCONSTANCY IN RELATIONSHIPS

She admitted that she had prayed every morning for a year that he would die. It's not right, Kirk thought, that District Attorneys will only prosecute solicitation for murder if God is NOT the one being solicited. Solicit a man to kill your husband? Go to jail. Solicit God to kill your husband? You skate. What a rip-off, huh? Compelling, also, the way things can shift: from stranger to acquaintance to friend to lover to spouse to enemy to . . . corpse, if her God—typically more available to her beck and call—had allowed her to have her way.

TOLERANCE

. . . His lesson in Applied Tolerance came during time spent with Grandmother and his grandfather. They modeled such tolerance perfectly. The grandfather went to church every Sunday, serving as the choir director; Grandmother went into the woods every Sunday, exercising some kind of communion of her own. They never questioned the other's practice; they never challenged the other's beliefs; they never tried to change the other. They did what they did separately and felt just fine; and they did what they did together and felt just fine. Applied Tolerance. No judging. Total acceptance. Unconditional Love.

HIS SPIRITUAL QUEST

In his energy-consuming search for salvation, he'd been dipped, dunked, sprayed, spayed, sprinkled, and neutered; in the quest for truth, he'd been blessed, cursed, cussed, lectured, scolded, and praised; in his pursuit of Life's Meaning, he'd been communion'd, Om'd, grape-juiced, wined, ahsram'd, accepted, rejected, Mu'd, and yoga'd . . .

Life

Some days, the pain in the body or in the mind seems to be so great that one must rest in order to heal. On awakening, one can live in peace as if all is well. So it is with what some call 'life': PAIN, HEALING, AWAKENING, and PEACE.

What Readers Are Saying About

The Twice-Stolen Necklace Murders

"*The Twice-Stolen Necklace Murders* is a 'wonderful Slaughterhouse for the Sacred Cows' of this culture. It should have been opened for business years ago. I felt like I was living with the weight of the world on my shoulders, when the real burden was from carrying around all those cows in my mind."

"This book freed me. I was locked into a state of self-inquiry and playing 'helper' and 'savior' to others, and that was taking a toll on me that I could not see. Freedom now is freedom from roles and from seeking to know more and from letting others 're-program' me. I'm at peace now, seeing I didn't need more knowledge and more programming but needed freedom from past programming."

"This book showed me that I can reach *Part Four* in the novel—the Peace state—only if I give up all the things I was so proud of and that I was willing to fight about: my city, my state, my country, my leaders, my group, my religion, my beliefs which were really their beliefs, my parents' values, all the 'my stuff' vs. 'their stuff.' What a lesson! I can be at peace if I give up the concepts I fought for!"

"I found out why I felt empty, even when I had it all."

"The work is a no-holds-barred challenge to those who would discriminate against others with different beliefs or along racial, gender, economic, and religious (or <u>no</u>-religion) lines. It is a call for tolerance and peace and is a step-by-step guide for attaining such peace on an individual basis."

"You've heard 'It'll make you laugh—it'll make you cry'? *The Twice-Stolen Necklace Murders* really made me laugh and made me cry."

"If you've ever said, *I don't even know who I am,* or if you have ever asked, *What is this all about?* or *Where did I really come from, where am I going, and what is the meaning of all this in between?* then you have a source that can give you the answer. This book is it."

Please visit us at:

www.markdhouston.com
and
www.floydhenderson.com

Prayer will not suspend or change the laws of nature. No super-natural power is going to do that.

NOTES

NOTES

NOTES

Notes

NOTES

NOTES

NOTES

Four Fulfillness   S E M B

Body   M E S B

Mind

Emotion

Spirit

CPSIA information can be obtained at www.ICGtesting.com
Printed in the USA
LVOW11s0454031113

359764LV00002B/400/A